Eleanor Roosevelt

Eleanor Roosevelt

Kem Knapp Sawyer

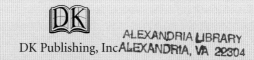

DK Publishing, Inc.

LONDON, NEW YORK, MUNICH,
MELBOURNE, and DELHI

Editors : Stephanie Smith, Beth Hester
Associate Editor : Alisha Niehaus
Editorial Assistant : John Searcy
Publishing Director : Beth Sutinis
Designer : Mark Johnson Davies
Senior Designer : Tai Blanche
Art Director : Dirk Kaufman
Photo Research : Anne Burns Images
Production : Ivor Parker
DTP Designer : Kathy Farias

First American Edition, 2006

06 07 08 09 10 10 9 8 7 6 5 4 3 2 1
Published in the United States
by DK Publishing, Inc.
375 Hudson Street, New York, New York 10014

DK books are available at special discounts for bulk purchases for sales
promotions, premiums, fund-raising, or educational use.
For details, contact:
DK Publishing Special Markets
375 Hudson Street, New York, NY 10014
SpecialSales@dk.com

A catalog record for this book is available
from the Library of Congress.

Color reproduction by GRB Editrice, Italy
Printed and bound in China by
South China Printing Co., Ltd.

Photography credits:
Cover Photo by Corbis/Marvin Koner
Back Cover Photo by Corbis/Bettman

Discover more at
www.dk.com

Contents

Chapter 1
Little Nell
6–7

CHAPTER 2
Granny
8–11

CHAPTER 3
"Thinking of You Always"
12–17

CHAPTER 4
Living with Grandmother Hall
18–25

CHAPTER 5
A Taste of Independence
26–31

CHAPTER 6
Volunteer and Debutante
32–37

CHAPTER 7
"Happiness!"
38–43

CHAPTER 8
Family, Friends, and Politics
44–51

CHAPTER 9
Fever at Campobello
52–55

Chapter 10
Courage
56–61

CHAPTER 11
Teacher, Writer, and
First Lady of New York
62–67

CHAPTER 12
The New Deal
68–75

CHAPTER 13
"The Trouble I've Seen"
76–83

CHAPTER 14
World at War
84–93

Chapter 15
A New Calling
94–101

CHAPTER 16
Life as an Adventure
102–107

CHAPTER 17
"You Learn by Living"
108–117

CHAPTER 18
"Her Glow Had Warmed
the World"
118–121

Timeline 122–123
Bibliography 124–125
Index 126
Organizations of Interest 127

chapter 1

Little Nell

When Eleanor was only eight years old, her mother died. Because their father was away, Eleanor and her two little brothers went to live with their grandmother. Eleanor couldn't wait for her father to return. She wanted so much to climb into his lap.

A few days later Eleanor was summoned to the library. In the dim light she saw her father, dressed in black, sitting in the big chair. "Little Nell," he called out. She ran to him, and he gathered her into his arms.

Eleanor's father, Elliott Roosevelt, looked very sad. Her mother, Anna, had meant all the world to him. Now that she was gone, he had only Little Nell and her two brothers. Someday, he told Eleanor, they would all be together. Little Nell would make a home for them. But for now the children would have to stay with their grandmother. Her father wanted his Little Nell to be good, study hard, and write often. He would try to visit whenever possible.

Elliott had always liked adventure. Before he was married he was an active sportsman who traveled to far-away places. He could charm anyone with his stories. But Eleanor liked him most of all because he had always made her feel special.

After her father left, Eleanor felt all alone in her grandmother's big house. Her grandmother was very strict. She made Eleanor follow many rules and insisted she wear old-fashioned clothes—flannel petticoats, long black stockings, and high-button shoes. But Eleanor never complained.

Eleanor waited patiently for her father to return. Sometimes she did not hear what people around her said, for she lived in a dream world where her father was her hero.

Little did Eleanor know she would grow up to be one of the world's most accomplished women, a first lady who would change the course of history. She would work with her husband, President Franklin D. Roosevelt, to bring the country out of the Depression and to lead it through a world war. As a speaker, a writer, and a public figure, she would work to end discrimination and promote civil rights. She would become a champion of international human rights, spreading goodwill wherever she traveled. Throughout her life, Little Nell would always be a friend to the downtrodden.

Little Nell looked forward to visits from the father she adored.

2

Granny

The world would call him "Greatheart." Theodore Roosevelt, Eleanor's grandfather, was born in 1831. He became a wealthy businessman and philanthropist in New York City, helping to found the Metropolitan Museum of Art and the American Museum of Natural History. One of the first New Yorkers to concern himself with the city's slums and neglected children, he helped establish the Newsboys Lodging House to provide homeless boys with warm beds. He provided financial support and also took time to counsel the boys.

His good deeds did not end there. After visiting an institution for the mentally ill, Theodore worked to improve its miserable conditions and insisted that patients be given the opportunity to work outdoors. In addition, he started the New

Theodore Roosevelt, Eleanor's grandfather, helped found the Metropolitan Museum of Art in New York City.

PHILANTHROPIST

Philanthropists devote time, energy, and money to charitable causes. In the late 19th century, philanthropists established organizations to care for the poor, the sick, and the mentally disabled.

York Orthopedic Hospital for the treatment of children suffering from deformities, such as misshapen legs or curved spines.

Theodore was well known for his good work. But he also enjoyed having a good time. He loved parties and was often the last to leave the dance floor.

In 1853 Theodore married Martha Bulloch, a southern belle

Theodore Roosevelt, stern but caring, wanted his children to live up to his high standards.

from Georgia. They had four children. Elliott, the third child, was afraid of the dark and was given to headaches and dizzy spells. He struggled to keep up with his older brother Teddy, who was an excellent student. Elliott attended St. Paul's, a New England boarding school, but only briefly. His nervous condition caused him to leave school. His father thought a rough outdoor experience would help cure him. Elliott was sent to Texas, where he learned to ride and hunt. He enjoyed the outdoor life and never went to college. After his father died, Elliott used part of his inheritance to travel the world. He made a hunting

expedition to India and became one of the first Americans to see Tibet.

Elliott returned from his travels for his sister's wedding and soon met 19-year-old Anna Hall, a gorgeous New York debutante. Anna was the oldest of six children and, like her father, was deeply religious. Her father supervised her reading and her daily activities, and even instructed her to walk with a stick across her back, fastened in the crook of her elbows, in an effort to improve her posture.

Eleanor's mother, Anna Hall Roosevelt, loved parties. She also directed skits for the Amateur Comedy Club.

A dashing young man, Elliott courted Anna, bringing her flowers and inviting her to join him on riding and boating outings. He proposed at a Memorial Day house party and the two were married on December 1, 1883. The *New York Times* called their wedding "one of the most brilliant" of the season.

Elliott and Anna led a glamorous social life, frequently attending polo matches, dances, and midnight suppers. They played tennis, sailed, and swam. All their friends

DEBUTANTE

At the time Eleanor was growing up, many upper class women often became debutantes at age 18. They attended dances and parties to show that they were ready to "come out" into society and were eligible for marriage.

Polo is a game played on horseback. Two teams use a long-handled mallet to hit a wooden ball into the goal.

thought this stunning young couple would have a wonderful future.

Their first daughter was born on October 11, 1884. They named her Anna Eleanor and called her Eleanor. To Elliott she was a "miracle from Heaven." When she was a little girl, Eleanor liked dancing for her father. She would twirl around and around until he picked her up and held her high in the air. He was the love of her life.

Although Elliott made Eleanor perfectly happy, her mother made her feel awkward and uncomfortable. From a very young age, Eleanor thought her mother was one of the most beautiful women she had ever seen, and that she was an "ugly duckling" by comparison. Eleanor was embarrassed whenever her mother explained to visitors, "She is such a funny child, so old-fashioned that we always call her 'Granny.'" Eleanor didn't like being called "Granny"; she much preferred the nickname her father gave her: Little Nell.

Eleanor had blonde hair and blue eyes and was a shy, serious child.

chapter 3

"Thinking of You Always"

Eleanor's parents loved to travel. When Eleanor was still quite little, only two and a half, she and her parents set sail for England on the *S. S. Britannic*. Almost as soon as they departed, their ship collided with another boat. Several passengers were killed, but the Roosevelts escaped. It was a traumatic event, especially for Eleanor. Amid frantic screams, Anna and Elliott were lowered into a lifeboat. Then a sailor took Eleanor, dangled her over the lifeboat, and dropped her into her father's outstretched arms.

After that incident, the terrified little girl refused to go to sea. Her parents were game to try again, however. Although reluctant to leave Eleanor behind, they set sail a few days later, once more venturing to England. Eleanor stayed with relatives on a small farm, where she played with chickens and collected eggs for breakfast.

Upon his return from England, Elliott rode in an amateur circus for a charity event. He fell from his horse and broke his leg. Eleanor cried for hours when she saw her father suffering. The doctors prescribed morphine, a medication to ease the pain. Elliott took more than he needed and soon became dependent on it. He also began to drink heavily. While there were days when he could be genuinely charming, at other times he became depressed, angry, or suspicious. The birth of a son, Elliott Jr., did little to lift his spirits.

Elliott's behavior and unpredictable moods worried Anna. She thought a change in scenery might help him recuperate. The family started out again on an ocean voyage, this time arriving without mishap. The Roosevelts traveled to Germany where Elliott took baths in mineral waters in an effort to restore his health. They went on to Italy, and stopped first in Venice. Elliott took Eleanor along the canals in a canoe-like boat, called a gondola, and sang to her. Eleanor loved listening to his beautiful voice. They traveled to the volcano at Mount

Eleanor poses with her father at their country house in Hempstead, Long Island. Elliott came here often to hunt and play polo.

Vesuvius and threw pennies into the lava. They sailed in the sea and learned to catch crabs.

Only very rarely did Elliott grow annoyed with Eleanor. Once, while riding donkeys in Italy, they came to a steep slope. The five-year-old Eleanor was too frightened to go downhill. This irritated Elliott, and he told her so. Eleanor hated to hear the disappointment in her father's voice. From then on she tried very hard to be brave.

When they arrived in Paris, Elliott was again suffering from nervousness. He became so ill that he entered a sanitarium to recover. Meanwhile, Anna, who was pregnant, needed to rest. Elliott's sister, Auntie Bye, came to look after Anna and little Elliott while Eleanor, then six years old, was sent to live at a convent school.

Anna wanted her daughter to make friends, learn French, and develop fine manners at the convent school. But Eleanor had a difficult time fitting in. More than anything she wanted attention, so when everyone became quite alarmed after another girl swallowed a copper penny, Eleanor announced that she, too, had swallowed a penny. The sisters at the convent did not believe her and called for her mother. Anna scolded her daughter for lying and made Eleanor quite miserable. Her father was the only one who did not make her feel like a criminal. She knew he would love her no matter what she did.

Soon after the birth of a new baby, a little boy named Hall,

Anna sailed with the children back to America. Elliott stayed behind in the sanitarium. Anna did not want to leave her husband, but Elliott's brother Ted had insisted it was for the best and she finally consented.

That winter, Anna and the three children lived in New York City. In the summer they moved to Tivoli, Eleanor's grandmother's house on the Hudson River, north of the city. Eleanor, who slept in her mother's room, saw that Anna was suffering from terrible headaches. Night after night she rubbed her mother's head to try to make her feel better.

When Eleanor's great-aunt Maggie discovered that Eleanor could not sew or read, she became quite alarmed. Anna decided to set up a classroom on the top floor of her house and hired a teacher for Eleanor and a few other girls her age. Eleanor tried hard to please her mother. She learned to read and also memorized Bible verses. Yet her mother never seemed satisfied.

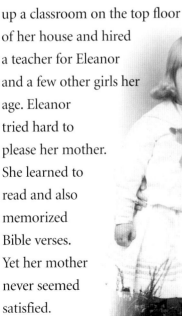

Eleanor, age seven, looked after her two brothers, two-year-old Elliott Jr. and baby Hall.

After many months, Elliott returned to New York. But he left again almost immediately, going first to Illinois to a center for the treatment of alcoholism, then to Virginia to continue his recovery. Nobody explained to Eleanor where he had gone. Sometimes, late at night, Anna and her two sisters, assuming Eleanor was asleep, would talk about Elliott and his troubles. Eleanor could not always understand the conversation or hear every word, but she knew that something was terribly wrong. She didn't dare ask her mother questions. Still, she wished someone would explain her father's mysterious absences and strange behavior.

The father Eleanor remembered was kind and thoughtful. She'd heard that, when Elliott was only seven, he'd given his new coat to a little

Eleanor spent much of her childhood at Tivoli, her grandmother's 14-bedroom house on the Hudson River.

boy who had no coat. He visited the newsboys and the children in the Orthopedic Hospital and could make them all laugh by telling funny stories. He was warm and affectionate to Eleanor. He made her feel loved.

On Eleanor's eighth birthday, Elliott wrote to his daughter, "I am thinking of you always and I wish for my Baby Girl the greatest Joy and the most perfect happiness in her sweet young life. Because Father is not with you is not because he doesn't love you." He added, "maybe soon I'll come back well and strong and we will have such good times together, like we used to have."

Not long after Elliott wrote this letter, Anna developed a high fever. The doctors diagnosed her illness as diphtheria. Eleanor's grandmother came to the house to take care of Anna. As the disease was very contagious, the children were sent away. The two boys went to stay with their great-aunt and Eleanor was taken in by her godmother, "Cousin Susie" Parish. Word was sent to notify Elliott, who had remained in Virginia.

The diphtheria quickly took its toll. Anna died on December 7, 1892, before Elliott was able to return to New York.

> ### Diphtheria
>
> Diphtheria is an infectious disease that causes difficulty breathing and swallowing. Until the late 19th century, it often resulted in death. In the 1890s, German doctor Emil Adolf Behring discovered an antitoxin vaccine for diphtheria. He received the Nobel Prize in medicine for his work in 1901. Babies in the United States are now immunized against this disease, and efforts are being made to immunize children all over the world.

chapter 4

Living with Grandmother Hall

Elliott did come home and he promised Eleanor they would spend time together. But soon he went away again, leaving the children with their grandmother. They were well taken care of in a household that included two aunts, two uncles, governesses, French maids, German maids, a cook, a butler, and a laundress.

Only five months after Anna died, both of Eleanor's brothers developed scarlet fever, a contagious disease. Eleanor was not allowed to be with other children. Once again she was sent to stay with her godmother, Cousin Susie. Eleanor felt comfortable living in Susie's house, but she was lonely. She enjoyed the long walks she took in the afternoon; still she missed playing with other children. She waited for her brothers to get better. Before long, Hall did recover, but young Elliott's

18

condition only worsened. He developed diphtheria, and died shortly thereafter.

This was more than Eleanor's father could bear. He spent even longer periods away from New York. Eleanor never stopped thinking about him. Whenever she heard the doorbell ring, she would rush to the top of the stairs to see if her father had returned. And if she caught sight of him coming through the door, she would slide down the banister into his arms.

Grandmother Hall paid close attention to Eleanor's education. She insisted Eleanor study French and music. Eleanor wanted more than anything to be a singer and thought this would make her father proud. She had always loved to listen to her father sing while Aunt Pussie played the piano. But unfortunately Eleanor could not carry a tune.

A generous man, Elliott loved to bring his children presents. He gave Eleanor two puppies, and there was even one Christmas when she received two stockings—one from her grandmother and one from her father. For her birthday, Elliott gave her a pony one year and her own saddle the next. Eleanor's aunts and uncles

Elliott took an interest in his children's education and suggested books for Eleanor to read.

19

taught her to ride and she caught on quickly. This delighted her father, who was an excellent horseman.

When Elliott visited, he would take Eleanor driving in a horse and cart. Mohawk, Elliott's frisky horse, liked to race madly through the streets of New York. Although Eleanor was usually timid, these rides with her father thrilled her. What upset her were the times her father said he would take her driving, but never appeared.

Elliott sent flowers on Easter and wrote letters all year long. He always called Eleanor "my darling Little Nell" or "my sweet Little Nell." He would ask her not to forget that he loved her dearly.

Eleanor received her first pony as a gift from her father. She would enjoy horseback riding all her life.

Sometimes he made up amusing stories and at other times he gave her advice. He urged her to do well in school. Once he explained that her brain was like an "education house" filled with funny little workmen carrying stones, or "facts." Many of these stones needed to be smoothed and polished. It was very important to make sure that teachers did not form crooked walls, but instead used "Persuasion, Instruction, Love, Truth, and Discipline" to build beautiful houses.

Eleanor's family had always encouraged her to spend time with those less fortunate. She accompanied her father to the Newsboys Lodging House, her grandfather's establishment for homeless boys, where children could come to play and eat. On Thanksgiving she and her father would help serve dinner. Every year she went with her grandmother to the babies' ward at a hospital to trim the Christmas tree. She also went with her Uncle Vallie to decorate a tree in Hell's Kitchen, one of the poorest slums in New York. Aunt Pussie and Aunt Maude took her to the Bowery Mission, a shelter for the homeless, where they would sing carols for all who gathered there.

Eleanor made special outings to the Orthopedic Hospital established by her grandfather. She visited with children who had to wear casts and splints, many of whom were unable to move for long periods of time. She took a special interest in these children because she herself had had to wear a steel brace to help cure a curvature of her spine.

On August 13, 1894, Elliott wrote to Eleanor that he had been ill and unable to move from his bed for days. He signed his letter, "with tender affection ever devotedly, Your Father Elliott Roosevelt." It was the last letter she received from him. Soon after, he drank excessively, fell, lost consciousness, and never woke up. After learning that her father had died, Eleanor cried herself to sleep. When she awoke the next day she refused to believe he was gone.

The funeral was arranged by Elliott's brother Ted, but Grandmother Hall did not let the children attend. The only memories Eleanor would carry with her were of a father who was gallant and brave, generous and kind, and whose love knew no bounds.

Eleanor and Hall's daily routine did not change. They still spent summers at Tivoli, a large

Eleanor watches her Aunt Maude go for a drive in a horse and buggy outside Tivoli.

Nantucket, an Island south of Cape Cod, Massachusetts, was once a center for whaling. It then became a popular holiday destination.

The Rainbow Fleet, Nantucket, Massachusetts

house with nine bedrooms as well as five rooms for servants. Since there was no gas or electricity in the house, the family used oil lamps and often went to bed by candlelight. Eleanor and her brother were allowed two hot baths a week.

Every morning Eleanor accompanied Grandmother Hall to the storeroom to weigh the flour, sugar, and coffee. Eleanor took supplies to the cook and then stopped to help Mrs. Overhalse with the washing and ironing. Madeleine, who helped look after the children, taught Eleanor to sew. Madeleine was hard to please, often ripping out Eleanor's handiwork and making her start over.

Eleanor enjoyed the company of her two aunts, Pussie and Maude, although Pussie was temperamental and might go for days without talking to anyone. Once, in the middle of the night, when Pussie was sick with a sore throat, she asked Eleanor to bring her some ice. Eleanor was scared of the dark, but she made her way down three flights of stairs and outside to fetch the ice. On another occasion, Pussie took Eleanor and her governess on a holiday to Nantucket Island. After a few days, Pussie left the hotel promising to return. She never

In the summer of 1899, at the age of 14, Eleanor was tall and slim. She had become more independent and was ready to start a new adventure.

kept her promise. Eleanor and her governess could not leave the hotel until Grandmother Hall sent them money to pay their hotel bill.

Aunt Pussie may have been unreliable, but she did provide adventure. She often played "I spy" with Eleanor. And sometimes, early in the morning, the two would wake up before anyone else, take bread and jam from the pantry, and set out by rowboat on the eight-mile journey into town to pick up the mail. When Eleanor's aunts and uncles were away, Eleanor had more time to dream and read. She would often take a book into the woods and sit under a tree. The library at Tivoli, filled with fiction as well as religious books, offered many choices.

Grandmother Hall gave Eleanor quite a bit of freedom, but she did have certain rules. She insisted Eleanor join her in morning and evening prayers. On Sundays Eleanor had to accompany her on the four-mile drive to church even though the ride left Eleanor sick to her stomach. After church the children were not allowed to play games and they always ate a cold supper. Dancing lessons were also required. Eleanor mastered the polka and the waltz and she studied ballet.

Eleanor and Hall looked forward to visiting Uncle Ted and Aunt Edith at Oyster Bay in Long Island, New York. The children played with their cousin Alice on the beach and went on picnics. Uncle Ted chased them through the haystacks. Sometimes he took them camping. He told them camping would teach them valuable lessons about people, such as who was willing to share the work.

As the years passed, visiting Alice made Eleanor increasingly uncomfortable. Alice was becoming not only good at sports, but also terribly sophisticated. She always wore fashionable clothes. Alice had an easy time talking with people her own age, but Eleanor felt shy and embarrassed in large groups. Eleanor was taller than the other girls her age and self-conscious about her height. She also had a bad habit of biting her nails.

Grandmother Hall decided Eleanor needed a change.

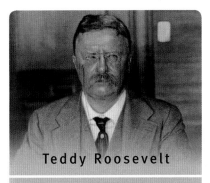

Teddy Roosevelt

Teddy Roosevelt first gained fame as the leader of the Rough Riders, a volunteer cavalry in the Spanish American War. A Republican, he was elected governor of New York in 1899 and vice president of the United States in 1900. Following the assassination of President William McKinley in 1901, Roosevelt became president. He was elected to serve a full term in 1904. While in office, he started the construction of the Panama Canal and worked to conserve natural resources and public lands.

chapter 5

A Taste of Independence

At the age of 15, Eleanor boarded the ship that would take her to England. She was a little nervous and very excited. Her great-aunt Tissie accompanied her on the ocean voyage and then took her to Allenswood, a school for girls just outside London. Marie Souvestre, the headmistress, was a pretty older woman with white hair that she wore pulled back in a twist. She had come from France and insisted that everyone speak French both in and out of class. Smart, strong-willed, and outspoken, the headmistress was greatly admired by her students and encouraged them to become independent thinkers.

All the girls followed a strict schedule with every hour planned. They woke early, made their beds, and then ate breakfast—rolls with butter and coffee with milk or chocolate.

Marie Souvestre, the headmistress of Allenswood, inspired her students to be inquisitive and imaginative, to think for themselves, to help others, and to become leaders.

Every morning their rooms were inspected. If the beds were not made well, all the sheets were removed and the offender had to start over. If the bureau drawers were not kept neat, all the contents were emptied onto the bed.

The students took a morning walk before attending classes. Eleanor studied English literature, history, and music, as well as French, German, Latin, and Italian. The headmistress taught history, Eleanor's favorite class, in her library, lecturing to students gathered around the fireplace.

Queen Victoria

In 1837, the 18-year-old Victoria was crowned Queen of England, becoming a formidable ruler of a vast empire. Eleanor witnessed the queen's funeral procession on the streets of London on February 2, 1901, and would never forget the deep emotions of the crowd. The Victorian period was a time of strict morality, when "children were to be seen and not heard." Eleanor's education at Allenswood allowed her to question these values for the first time.

Physical exercise followed lunch. (One of the proudest moments of Eleanor's life was when she made the field hockey team.) At four o'clock, the girls were given thick slices of bread with butter and, on occasion, raspberry jam. After tea they studied until the bell rang to announce that it was time to dress for dinner.

27

Eleanor wrote of her years at Allenswood, "I really marvel now at my confidence and independence, for I was totally without fear in this new phase of my life."

At dinner Eleanor was assigned a special place at Marie Souvestre's table. Afterward, Marie often invited Eleanor and a few other students to her study. They spent the evenings reading aloud poems or plays in French. Eleanor enjoyed the company of the teachers and the other students. She was well liked in her new school. It seemed so much easier to make friends there than it had been at home.

Eleanor became quite confident in her new skills. Allenswood was strict and the headmistress demanding, yet Eleanor had never experienced such happiness. Not that the school or the English climate was perfect. Eleanor wished the girls were allowed more than three baths a week.

And she found that most of the school year was cold and foggy. The only way to get warm was to sit on the radiator.

Eleanor traveled many places during her school vacations. She went to Paris for Christmas and bought a dark red dress, the most beautiful dress she had ever owned. She wore it on Sundays and during the evening and never grew tired of it. One summer, her great-aunt Tissie invited her to visit the Alps.

On Easter, Marie Souvestre took Eleanor back to France and also to Italy, introducing her to historic sites, magnificent scenery, and new foods. She let Eleanor explore cities on her own, guidebook in hand. She asked Eleanor to buy the train tickets, handle the luggage, and make most of the arrangements. Eleanor was thrilled with the responsibility. Eleanor had always assumed one made plans and stuck to them, but Marie had other ideas about travel. Once, on a train to Pisa, she heard the conductor announce the next stop, Alassio.

Allenswood School attracted girls from several European countries as well as America.

This painting by Eugene Auguste Francois Deully depicts the color and romance of Paris, a city Eleanor visited during her school vacations.

Remembering she had a friend in Alassio, Marie suddenly hopped off the train, Eleanor in tow.

Marie encouraged Eleanor to be more free spirited and taught her to be a citizen of the world. She inspired Eleanor to continue her study of foreign languages so she could speak them on her travels. And she gave her great confidence that she could handle new situations.

Eager to encourage independence, Marie had allowed Eleanor to wander the streets of Paris alone. But when word got back to Grandmother Hall that Eleanor was unchaperoned, Grandmother Hall was so upset she made Eleanor leave the school. So, two years after arriving at Allenswood, Eleanor sailed home with Aunt Pussie and spent a trying summer at Tivoli. Aunt Pussie called her an "ugly duckling" and also told her far more about her father's troubled life than she had ever known. Eleanor was miserable and longed to return to Allenswood in the fall.

After much coaxing, Grandmother Hall relented. Eleanor arrived at school thrilled to be back. The headmistress, her other teachers, and her friends were all happy to see her. Once again Eleanor enjoyed her independence. She liked knowing she was accepted. No one made her feel she wasn't good enough, smart enough, or pretty enough to do what she wanted. She could go into London for weekends, and on her vacations she traveled to France and Italy.

Eleanor returned to America in the summer of 1902. She was sorry to leave both the school and Marie Souvestre. With the exception of her father, Marie was the one person who had most influenced her. Marie would also miss Eleanor. On her final report card, the headmistress wrote that Eleanor "had the most admirable influence on the school and gained the affection of many, the respect of all. To me personally I feel I lose a dear friend indeed."

Eleanor was spending a summer holiday in St. Moritz, Switzerland, with her great-aunt Tissie when this photograph was taken. She loved the little cafés where she and her aunt would sit and drink hot chocolate.

6

Volunteer and Debutante

When Eleanor returned home, her brother Hall was 12. Like many boys from his social class, he was sent to boarding school. Both Grandmother Hall and Eleanor took Hall to Groton School in Massachusetts. More and more responsibility for Hall would now fall to Eleanor. Grandmother Hall, growing more reclusive with age, never returned to Groton. It was Eleanor who kept in touch, writing letters and visiting her brother on weekends.

Theodore Roosevelt, Eleanor's Uncle Ted, had become president. His daughter Alice had already made her debut in the White House. Grandmother Hall was eager for Eleanor to make her debut with the other 18-year-olds from New York society. She arranged for Eleanor to move into the family's New York City townhouse where Aunt Pussie was living. But Pussie was hardly a reliable chaperone. Courted by multiple suitors, Pussie filled her own

At age 18, Eleanor made her debut in New York City.

social calendar with dinners and dances. So much activity often proved more than she could handle. Pussie was given to emotional outbursts and would sometimes shut herself in her room and refuse to eat.

Eleanor attended her first ball at the Waldorf-Astoria, one of the most elegant hotels in New York City. But she felt so miserable and out of place that she left early. She hated thinking that everyone would compare her unfavorably to her mother, once the belle of the ball. Also, she was jealous of Aunt Pussie's beaus and her flirtatious cousin Alice's popularity. They never left the dance floor, while Eleanor longed to be back at Allenswood where she'd found it so

After leaving Allenswood, Eleanor was pulled in two directions. She longed to be accepted by New York society and she also wanted to work in the city's poorest neighborhoods.

much easier to make friends. Marie Souvestre still kept in touch with Eleanor and had written her that fall saying how helpful she would have been in welcoming the new students. "You would have known how to make them feel rapidly at ease, and happy in circumstances so different from their usual lives."

Still, Eleanor was convinced she needed to be accepted by New York society. So she continued to go to other parties. She enjoyed the company of Bob Ferguson, an old friend of the family, who often escorted her to and from dances. By the end of the year, Eleanor had made many friends, including her distant cousin, Franklin Delano Roosevelt.

James and Sara, Franklin's parents, had become good friends with Elliott, Eleanor's father, on an ocean voyage he made before he met Anna. They later asked Elliott to be their son's godfather. When Eleanor was only two she had accompanied her parents to Hyde Park, James and Sara's home on the Hudson River. While the adults talked, the children played in the nursery. Franklin pretended to be a horse and let Eleanor ride on his back. Later, when Franklin and Eleanor saw each other at family Christmas parties, Franklin told his mother that he admired Eleanor's mind.

Now Franklin was taking a romantic interest in Eleanor. He met her at a horse show, joined her for

Franklin Roosevelt was born in 1882 on his family's estate, a 15-room house at Hyde Park. It would remain his home throughout his lifetime.

lunch, and took her to tea. The new year was filled with special occasions: a trip to Washington to visit Uncle Ted in the White House, Franklin's 21st birthday celebration, and house parties at Hyde Park. Franklin and Eleanor went to the theater, played tennis, and took walks in the rain. That August, Eleanor visited Franklin and his mother at Campobello, an island in Canada, off the coast of Maine, where Franklin's mother had a summer cottage.

The following autumn, Eleanor started to work at the Rivington Street Settlement House in an immigrant neighborhood on the Lower East Side in New York City. Every afternoon she took a streetcar downtown to conduct classes for children. Eleanor taught calisthenics and dancing while her friend

Settlement House

The Roosevelts and others in their social set lived a comfortable, even glamorous, existence. But two-thirds of New York's population then lived in tenements, crowded apartments with unsanitary conditions found mostly in Lower Manhattan. Social reformers, mostly college-educated women, established, and often lived in, settlement houses in immigrant communities. There, children gathered for activities and parents took classes.

CALISTHENICS

Physical exercises designed to develop strength and grace.

Jean Reid played the piano. As the children grew to love her, Eleanor blossomed. One little girl liked Eleanor's classes so much that she begged Eleanor to come home with her so her father could give her teacher a present.

At the same time, Eleanor wanted to improve the hazardous conditions many people, especially women, faced at work. Factories lacked ventilation and decent lavatories, and some girls worked 12-14 hours a day, six days a week. Children as young as four were being put to work.

In the beginning of their relationship, Eleanor tried hard to please Sara, Franklin's mother.

Department store clerks were not allowed to take breaks. Eleanor joined the Consumers League, an organization established to correct these abuses. She visited clothing factories and department stores and wrote reports. What she saw deeply disturbed her and inspired her to support new reforms in labor laws.

Eleanor still found time to visit Franklin, who was in his last year at Harvard College near Boston.

After Sara asked them to delay their wedding plans, Eleanor and Franklin remained secretly engaged for more than a year.

Franklin was studying history and government and was also editor-in-chief of the *Crimson*, the college newspaper. In November 1903, Eleanor joined Franklin for the Harvard-Yale football game and then went to Groton School to visit her brother. The next day Franklin followed her to Groton. That afternoon he asked Eleanor to marry him.

Eleanor was thrilled and accepted Franklin's proposal. A few days later, she wrote him a letter including lines from a poem by Elizabeth Barrett Browning, "Unless you can swear, 'For life, for death!' Oh, fear to call it loving!"

But Sara, Franklin's mother, thought Eleanor and Franklin were far too young to contemplate marriage. Sara had lost her husband in 1900. She was not prepared to lose her only son, too.

chapter 7

"Happiness!"

Eleanor and Franklin both shared a common ancestor, Claes van Rosenvelt, a Dutchman who had settled in the New World in 1649. The Roosevelts made their homes in New Amsterdam (which later became New York City) and in the surrounding countryside in New York state. In 1880, Franklin's father, James, a 52-year-old wealthy businessman, married the 26-year-old Sara Delano. Sara was born at Algonac, the Delano estate on the Hudson River, but spent part of her youth in China. Sara came from a long line of sea captains, and her father had made his fortune in the shipping trade.

Sara and James returned from a 10-month honeymoon in Europe to the beautiful rolling hills of Hyde Park, James's large New York estate. Franklin was born there on January 30, 1882.

As Franklin grew older, both his parents encouraged him to develop his many hobbies: He collected stamps, enjoyed horseback riding, played tennis, and took piano lessons. He took to the water in summer and winter, mastering

When Franklin was little, his father taught him to sail the *Half Moon*, a 51-foot (15.5 meter) yacht.

sailboats and ice boats. With few playmates, he became an avid reader. History and the sea were his favorite subjects.

Franklin was taught by governesses until the age of 14, when his parents sent him to boarding school at Groton. An average student, he studied Latin, Greek, history, and literature. He excelled at the high kick, a sport that involved both leaping and kicking. Groton's headmaster, Reverend Endicott Peabody, who inspired many of his students to choose public service as a career, took a special interest in Franklin. After graduation, Franklin went on to attend Harvard College.

This photograph of Franklin and his parents, James and Sara, was taken in 1901, the year before James's death.

While Franklin was a freshman, his father died. Sara had always doted on Franklin. With her husband gone, she drew even closer to Franklin, taking a keen interest in everything he did and even renting an apartment in Boston to be close to him.

But nothing Sara said could make Franklin less determined to marry Eleanor. A letter to his mother read:

"Dearest Mama, I know what pain I must have caused you and you know I wouldn't do it if I really could have helped it...you know that nothing can ever change what we have always been and always will be to each other—only now you have two children to love and to love you—and Eleanor as you know will always be a daughter to you in every true way. Your ever loving F.D.R."

Nonetheless, Sara persuaded Franklin to postpone announcing the engagement for a year. During that year, Eleanor and Franklin wrote letters, exchanged poems, and visited each other. Still hoping her son would reconsider the marriage, Sara took Franklin on a five-week Caribbean cruise in January of 1904. But there was to be no change of plans. Franklin's mind was made up.

After his graduation from Harvard, Franklin enrolled at Columbia University Law School in New York and could see Eleanor more frequently. Sometimes he met her after work at the Rivington Street Settlement House and once he joined Eleanor in taking a sick child home. He was appalled by the conditions in the tenement and confessed to having had no idea people lived that way.

At 20, Eleanor made a beautiful bride, surprising many of her relatives who had once called her an "ugly duckling."

As a wedding present, Franklin gave Eleanor a watch with her initials engraved on it. The watch was attached to a pin bearing the Roosevelt family insignia of three feathers. Eleanor wore this pin throughout her life.

In December 1904 Franklin and Eleanor announced their engagement. Family and friends were thrilled; even Sara became resigned to it. Congratulations poured in. Theodore Roosevelt, Eleanor's uncle, recently elected to a second term as president, wrote to Franklin, "I am as fond of Eleanor as if she were my own daughter....No other success in life—not the Presidency or anything else—begins to compare with the joy and happiness that come in and from the love of a true man and a true woman." Eleanor accepted her uncle's offer to stand in for her father and give her away at the wedding.

The wedding took place on March 17, 1905, in Cousin Susie's home on 76th Street in New York City. All of Eleanor's aunts and cousins fussed over her as she dressed for the wedding. Aunt Pussie told her to drink strong tea to bring color to her cheeks. Marie Souvestre sent a telegram with the one word "Bonheur!" (French for "Happiness!")

Eleanor wore a long-sleeved white satin dress, her mother's veil, and a necklace of pearls and diamonds that was a gift from Sara. With a bouquet of lilies of the valley in her arms, she made a beautiful bride. The guests were amazed she was no longer the "ugly ducking" she had been called as a child.

Reverend Endicott Peabody, the head of Groton School, performed the ceremony. Eleanor and Franklin's close friends came up to congratulate them, but it was not long before the bride and groom were standing alone. The other two hundred guests had followed President Roosevelt into the library!

The young couple traveled to Hyde Park for a brief honeymoon. Then Franklin returned to law school to finish the term. They spent the summer on a second honeymoon in Europe. Aboard ship they danced, dined, walked on deck, and played endless rounds of piquet, a two-person card game. In London, they were given the royal suite at Brown's Hotel after they were mistaken for President Roosevelt and his wife. Eleanor and Franklin traveled from there to Paris, Milan, and Venice. Wherever they went,

While on their honeymoon, Franklin, an avid photographer, took this picture of Eleanor on a gondola in Venice, Italy.

Franklin insisted they shop for books and prints. They also fed the pigeons at St. Mark's Square in Venice and enjoyed gondola rides along the canals.

They toured Germany and the Alps before ending their honeymoon on the Scottish moors. There they visited the family of Eleanor's good friend, Bob Ferguson. At tea one afternoon, their hostess Lady Helen asked Eleanor to tell her the difference between the national and state governments in the United States. Eleanor could not begin to explain the difference. Terribly embarrassed, she vowed to learn more about her own government.

When the newlyweds returned to New York they discovered that Sara had found them a house on 36th Street, only a few blocks from her own home. It appeared that everything had already been prepared. The servants were hired and the house furnished. Eleanor's new life had started, but she had made few decisions about it on her own.

National and State Governments

The United States operates under a federal system of government: Power is shared by the national government—the president and Congress—and state governments—governors and state legislatures. Other countries, such as Britain and France, have a unitary system of government where the central government exercises all the power. Proponents of a federal system believe that it allows more opportunities for different voices to be heard. Critics maintain that this system allows states to pass laws resulting in racial or economic discrimination.

8

Family, Friends, and Politics

Eleanor came from a privileged class and married into a family even more wealthy than her own. Sara was generous, and it appeared that the young couple would have all that money could buy. Yet what Eleanor wished for most was to feel loved and accepted. Her education at Allenswood and her work at the Rivington Street Settlement House had given her confidence. Still, she longed for attention and admiration. She had never lived up to her own mother's high expectations and now she was determined to forge a different relationship with her mother-in-law. Eleanor worked hard to win Sara's approval. They spent many an afternoon together, attending a luncheon or going for a drive.

Franklin and Eleanor's first baby was born on May 3, 1906. She was named

When Eleanor was first married she relied on Sara. She later wrote, "I was beginning to be an entirely dependent person."

Anna and was soon followed by a baby boy. Born on December 23, 1907, James was named for Sara's husband. As was the custom among the upper class, the Roosevelts hired a nurse to take charge of the babies' care and discipline. Eleanor rarely expressed her opinions on childrearing, but she did insist on fresh air. In fact, she sometimes placed Anna in a box that she hung outside from a back window! She kept up the practice until Anna screamed so loudly that a neighbor complained about inhumane treatment.

The Roosevelts spent much of their time at Sara's house in Hyde Park. Here Eleanor is holding nine-month-old James and two-year-old Anna.

After James was born, Sara decided her son's family needed more room. She bought a plot of land on East 65th Street in New York and had two narrow houses built side by side, one for herself and one for Franklin and Eleanor. The houses were designed so that the drawing rooms and dining rooms could open onto each other for large parties. Sara and Franklin made all the plans concerning the construction of the houses. Eleanor was not consulted, nor did she show any great interest.

Most of the time Eleanor did not admit even to herself that she had lost the independence that once was hers.

Eleanor suffered greatly after her baby son, Franklin Jr., died. She kept this portrait of him on her bureau.

But shortly after moving into the new house, she sat down at her dressing table and wept. When Franklin found her she told him that she did not like living in a house that she did not feel was her own.

Eleanor recovered and soon fell back into her usual pattern of keeping her feelings to herself. She spent long hours knitting and doing embroidery. She took lessons in French, Italian, and German. Like Franklin, she read extensively.

Baby Franklin was born on March 18, 1909. He died before he was eight months old from a complication of the flu. He was buried in the churchyard at Hyde Park on November 7. Eleanor blamed herself for his death. She was haunted by the thought that if she had relied less on others and cared more for her baby herself, her son might have lived.

The birth of a new baby boy on September 23, 1910, was a joyful event. He was named Elliott for Eleanor's father. That same year, Franklin left his law practice and entered his first political race, campaigning as a Democrat for the New York state senate. He rented a bright red car and set out

to visit every small village in the state, becoming the first politician to make use of the automobile.

After Franklin won the election, the Roosevelts moved to Albany, the state capital of New York. For the first time they chose and furnished their own home without Sara's help. Eleanor found that she rather enjoyed it.

Eleanor also discovered she shared Franklin's devotion to public service. She savored discussing and debating the topics of the day with him. It surprised her to learn that Franklin was supporting women's suffrage. At the time, most male politicians opposed women's suffrage, and she herself did not yet fully embrace the cause. Eleanor had grown up in a family where it was always assumed that men knew more about politics than women. Now she started to question those views.

A newspaperman named Louis Howe believed in Franklin's future and soon became his top adviser. During his reelection

Women's Suffrage

The campaign for women's suffrage, or the right of women to vote, began in 1848 when Elizabeth Cady Stanton and Lucretia Mott made the Declaration of the Rights of Women at Seneca Falls, New York. In 1869 Susan B. Anthony advocated an amendment to the Constitution providing for women's suffrage. After a long struggle, the Nineteenth Amendment was approved in 1920, granting women the right to vote.

campaign for state senate, Franklin was stricken with typhoid fever and asked Louis to run his campaign. Eleanor at first did not think much of Louis; she detested his cigarette smoking and his untidy manner. It especially annoyed her that Louis would smoke while he was consulting Franklin, who was still weak and bedridden. But Louis's political sense was sharp. His advice paid off and Franklin won the race.

Franklin never served a full second term. President Woodrow Wilson appointed him assistant secretary of the navy, and the family moved to Washington, D.C. Louis Howe became Franklin's assistant. Eleanor was expected to visit the wives of public officials, sometimes as many as 30 in one day. She had always fulfilled her obligations, and this would be no exception. She visited the Supreme Court wives on Monday, the Congressional

This family portrait shows (from left to right) Elliott, Franklin, Franklin Jr., James, Eleanor holding John, and Anna. It was taken in 1916 while the family lived in Washington, D.C.

wives on Tuesday, Cabinet wives on Wednesday, wives of Senators on Thursday, and wives of diplomats on Fridays. The more visits she made, the less shy she became. Eleanor became so busy that she hired a social secretary, a young, competent, and attractive woman named Lucy Mercer.

Eleanor and Franklin also dined out with friends and held informal Sunday evening suppers at their house. Eleanor kept the meals simple: She made scrambled eggs and served

World War I

In World War I, the Central Powers—Germany, Austria-Hungary, and Turkey—fought against the Allies—France, Great Britain, Russia, Italy, Japan, and the United States. With the introduction of poisonous gases and air bombings, the war became the bloodiest world had yet experienced. Ten million people were killed, and twice that number were wounded.

cold meat, salad, dessert and cocoa. While Franklin was stationed in Washington, two more children were born: the second Franklin on August 17, 1914, and John, on March 13, 1916. The Roosevelts moved from their small house on N Street to a larger one on R Street with a garden in the back. Eleanor now spent more time caring for her youngest children and relied less on baby nurses. In the summers she took all the children to Campobello Island where they could swim, picnic, and go boating.

SHELL-SHOCKED

Shell-shocked soldiers suffer nervous breakdowns from exposure to battle.

In 1914, the assassination of the Archduke of Austria-Hungary sparked World War I. The United States did not enter the war until April 16, 1917. As assistant secretary to the navy, Franklin needed to prepare the navy for battle. While young men were shipped overseas, women organized to help the war effort at home.

Eleanor volunteered to work at the Red Cross canteen to provide food for troops and workers. She did everything from mopping floors to making sandwiches and coffee. She brought flowers, candy, and newspapers to the wounded men in the naval hospital, many of them shell-shocked. She visited St. Elizabeth's Hospital and, appalled by the miserable conditions there, convinced the secretary of the interior to increase the hospital's funding. She helped organize entertainment for the troops. She distributed free wool to other volunteers and, whenever she had a free moment, she knit gifts for the sailors. There were days when she started at 9 AM and did not return home until 1 AM. Eleanor received tremendous satisfaction from her work, just as she had at the Rivington Street Settlement House.

In July 1918, Franklin was sent overseas to escort naval ships to France and to tour the war zone. In September, Eleanor was handed a telegram informing her that Franklin had pneumonia and was returning home. She was to bring a doctor and ambulance to meet her husband at the dock.

What developed would shake Eleanor to the core. In unpacking her husband's belongings, Eleanor found love

letters from Lucy Mercer. The discovery stunned her. She had never suspected that her husband was unfaithful. Eleanor was profoundly hurt and offered Franklin a divorce.

But Franklin did not accept Eleanor's offer and they agreed to stay married. They would try to work things out. Still, Eleanor lost some of the self-confidence she had recently gained. She could not erase the pain she had experienced. Several times a week she would drive to Rock Creek Cemetery in Washington where, sitting on a stone bench, she would find comfort gazing at *Grief*, the statue of a cloaked figure. She was re-examining her life and gaining the strength to carry on.

Author Henry Adams, after his wife Clover committed suicide, commissioned the statue known as *Grief* to be built by sculptor Augustus Saint-Gaudens. Clover had learned that her husband was in love with another woman.

chapter 9

Fever at Campobello

After the peace agreement, signed on November 11, 1918, brought an end to World War I, Americans took to the streets to celebrate. In January, Franklin and Eleanor left the children behind to tour the battlefields and war-torn countryside in Europe. Eleanor was appalled by the devastation. The more she saw, the more convinced she became that the world must find peaceful ways to resolve its conflicts.

James M. Cox campaigned with Franklin, his vice-presidential candidate, in the 1920 election.

Sara, Franklin, Eleanor, and the children spent summers on Campobello Island, off the coast of Maine. Sara lived in a cottage next door to Eleanor and Franklin.

In 1920, James M. Cox became the Democratic nominee for president, and Franklin was chosen as his running mate. After Eleanor took their oldest son James to Groton School, where he would follow in his father and uncle's footsteps, she joined Franklin on a four-week campaign trip. But James Cox and Franklin lost the election to the Republican candidate, Warren Harding. Franklin then resumed his law practice in New York. Eleanor also took an interest in women's political rights, volunteering for the League of Women Voters. Female suffragists had started this new organization to help women, who had just gained the right to vote, undertake their new responsibilities.

In the summer, the Roosevelts left the heat behind and traveled to Campobello Island for the cool, refreshing air. One afternoon in August 1921, they were returning from a sailing trip when they saw a forest fire. They immediately headed for shore to put out the fire. Afterward, Franklin and the children jogged two miles and then took a dip in the icy waters. Later, Franklin, still in his bathing suit, sat down to read the mail. He started to feel a chill and went to bed early.

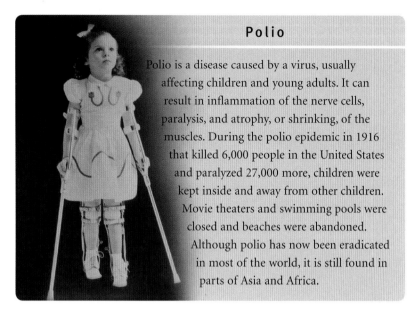

Polio

Polio is a disease caused by a virus, usually affecting children and young adults. It can result in inflammation of the nerve cells, paralysis, and atrophy, or shrinking, of the muscles. During the polio epidemic in 1916 that killed 6,000 people in the United States and paralyzed 27,000 more, children were kept inside and away from other children. Movie theaters and swimming pools were closed and beaches were abandoned. Although polio has now been eradicated in most of the world, it is still found in parts of Asia and Africa.

By the next morning Franklin had developed a fever and his legs ached. Eleanor consulted doctors in the area. One of them thought Franklin was suffering from a blood clot and recommended massage. Eleanor sent the children on a camping trip so she could use all her energy to care for Franklin. Franklin lost control of his left leg, and then his right. Eleanor was worried, but all the while she tried to remain cheerful to keep Franklin's spirits up. She nursed him, bathed him, brought him meals, and entertained him; still Franklin's legs remained paralyzed. Eleanor and Franklin drew strength from each other and showed great courage in believing Franklin would overcome his illness.

Dr. Lovett, a specialist from Newport, Rhode Island, was

summoned to give his opinion. He determined that Franklin had contracted infantile paralysis, also called polio. The leg massages had only increased the already severe pain. Dr. Lovett recommended that Franklin be moved to a New York hospital. Much would depend on Franklin's will to recover.

Louis Howe had arrived and did all he could to assist Eleanor and encourage Franklin. Eleanor had grown fond of Louis in recent years. She recognized how much he had helped her develop her own political skills during the vice-presidential campaign. She had also come to appreciate the depth of Louis's devotion to Franklin. Louis took over Franklin's mail and, as the days wore on, his responsibilities increased. No matter how ill Franklin appeared, Louis never lost hope of Franklin's bright political future.

As soon as Franklin was strong enough, Louis arranged to transport him to New York. Franklin was taken by boat to the railway station and placed in a private car. Louis wanted as few people as possible to know about Franklin's infirmity. He arranged for an ambulance to meet the train, but kept secret the identity of the man strapped to the stretcher.

The Salk Vaccine

Physician and medical researcher Jonas Salk, born in New York City, discovered a vaccine to combat polio. This development was announced on April 12, 1955, the 10th anniversary of Franklin Roosevelt's death. In the next four years, 450 million doses were administered. In 1994, the western hemisphere was declared free of polio.

10

Courage

Franklin remained in the hospital until just before Christmas. Louis tried to keep the story out of the papers. Meanwhile, Franklin's family showered him with attention. James was away at Groton, but the other Roosevelt children visited him every day after school.

Eleanor, patient and hopeful, continued to care for Franklin after he returned home. Each day Franklin was made to stretch his muscles a bit more. It was hard work, but he bore the pain courageously.

By spring Franklin was sitting on the floor and playing with

Eleanor often held political meetings and dinners at her home on 65th Street in New York City. She is shown here with Louis Howe seated to her right.

his younger children.
The older ones had a
harder time accepting the
changes in their father.
Anna, now 14, became

especially unhappy. She resented her mother for treating her like a child. When her grandmother Sara questioned why Louis, who had come to live with them, was given the better room, Anna grew even more angry.

Both Eleanor and Louis urged Franklin to return to politics. Sara, however, felt this would be far too difficult for Franklin. He needed rest, and the more rest the better. Sara wanted him to retire to Hyde Park. Franklin was torn: He loved politics with a passion. But he was in pain and was not sure he would ever walk again. He did not know how much strength he had. If he were to make the necessary sacrifice to run for office, he wanted a good shot at winning. And success was not assured.

In the end, Eleanor and Louis prevailed. They convinced Franklin that, with time and proper planning, he could win an elected office. Engaging his mind with what mattered most to him would give him the motivation to regain his strength.

Louis also persuaded Eleanor that her own involvement in politics would help Franklin. Eleanor became friends with Marion Dickerman, who was active in the Women's Trade Union League. Social reformers, including settlement house workers and trade union members, had founded the League to improve working conditions for women. Eleanor raised badly

Eleanor and her friends Nancy Cook, Caroline O'Day, and Marion Dickerman gave speeches, raised funds, and published a newspaper to support the women's division of the Democratic State Committee.

needed funds, taught classes in current events, and, with the help of her own children, hosted a Christmas party for the families of League members.

Marion's friend Nancy Cook persuaded Eleanor to support the women's division of the Democratic State Committee. Eleanor gave her first speech in front of a large group. She spent many evenings in her friends' apartments in New York's Greenwich Village discussing politics and women's rights, as well as working on a newspaper published by the Democratic State Committee.

Louis helped Eleanor become a better public speaker. He taught her to stop her nervous habit of giggling and encouraged her to lower her voice so she could be heard from a distance. He told her to smile and breathe deeply if she became nervous. And, most importantly, he instructed her to avoid rambling: "Have something you want to say, say it, and sit down."

In the summer, Eleanor took the children to Hyde Park and encouraged them to enjoy the outdoors. She wanted to make sure the younger boys learned to swim, ride, and camp, even without a father to teach them. She often took the lead now, participating in activities she had shied away from early in her marriage. She enjoyed spending more time with Anna and tried to treat her more like an adult.

Convinced that swimming in warm water would help him make progress, Franklin traveled south in the winter. At first Eleanor accompanied him on houseboat cruises around the coast of Florida. But she was often cold and uncomfortable and did not like to fish. Franklin's secretary, Missy LeHand, took over the arrangements. Both Franklin and Eleanor came to rely increasingly on Missy.

Franklin developed broad shoulders and strong arms to compensate for his inability to use his legs. He enjoyed swimming and even played water polo. He also drove his own car, a Ford equipped with hand controls. It took great effort and determination on his part, but eventually he

Swimming helped Franklin (left) recuperate.

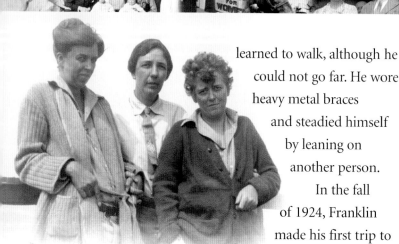

learned to walk, although he could not go far. He wore heavy metal braces and steadied himself by leaning on another person.

In the fall of 1924, Franklin made his first trip to Warm Springs, Georgia, a former spa with a pool fed by warm spring water. The water felt

Eleanor traveled to Campobello with her friends Marion Dickerman and Nancy Cook.

soothing and relaxing. Franklin started to dream of establishing a healing center for children with polio. In 1926, Franklin bought the run-down resort at Warm Springs and began to rebuild it. He invited polio-stricken children from around the world to enjoy the water at Warm Springs and participate in the games and exercises. He also built his own cottage where he would often spend several months of the winter. Eleanor and the children stayed behind in New York and visited on school holidays.

While Franklin was setting up the center at Warm Springs, Eleanor and her friends were pursuing their own dreams. Nancy Cook, Marion Dickerman, and Eleanor started a small factory to provide jobs for local farmers who were out of work. They hired master craftsmen to train apprentices to make reproductions of early American furniture. Eleanor and her friends chose a spot where they had often gone to picnic, by a brook called Val-Kill, not far from the house at Hyde Park. Franklin encouraged them and designed the buildings himself, a stone cottage where Nancy and Marion would live and, next door, the factory for their new business venture. Called Val-Kill Industries, this business would later expand to include a pewter workshop and a weaving program.

Devoted to her new political causes, Eleanor wrote articles for the *Women's Democratic News* and made public appearances throughout New York. Together with Nancy, Marion, and Elinor Morgenthau, a friend from Hyde Park, she toured the state to campaign for women's rights, including the right to serve on juries and the right to be represented in Democratic party committees. She also promoted child labor legislation and the 48-hour work week (in an era when 12-14 hour days and a six-day week were routine).

Eleanor had concerned herself with politics to help Franklin's future career, but she found she cared deeply about the issues facing America and enjoyed confronting them head-on. Now, she wanted to change the world.

Eleanor took a keen interest in the local carpenters' work at the Val-Kill furniture factory.

chapter **11**

Teacher, Writer, and First Lady of New York

Always full of energy, Eleanor started to teach in addition to working on political causes. She began in 1927 at Todhunter School for Girls, a private school in New York City, where Eleanor's friend Marion Dickerman was assistant principal. When Miss Todhunter, the principal, returned to England, she sold the school to Marion, Nancy Cook, and Eleanor. Marion became principal and Eleanor a teacher in the upper grades.

Just as Marie Souvestre had helped change Eleanor's life by encouraging her to think about her role in society and in the world, so, too, Eleanor wanted to inspire her students. She taught American history, English and American literature, drama, and current events. She brought students to the tenements near the Rivington Street Settlement House where she had once worked so they could see how

Eleanor worked long hours at her desk, composing articles, preparing exams, and working on political campaigns.

Current Events Test

Eleanor led her current events students on field trips throughout the city and engaged them in serious, thought-provoking discussions. Her exams included short answer and essay questions.

I. What do you think has been the most important international event in the last three months?

II. What do you think has been the most important event in this country in the field of business during the last three months?

III. What do you think has been the most important event in politics?

IV. What do you think has been the most important event in the scientific world?

different people lived. She took her class to visit the courts to learn firsthand how the justice system worked. Before long Eleanor became vice principal of the school.

With surprising frequency, Eleanor continued to make her voice heard. Her writing was clear, direct, and honest. She got straight to the point. In an article called "What I Want Most Out of Life," published in *Success* magazine in 1927, she shared her mission in life, stressing the importance of doing something useful.

In September 1928, Eleanor took John, their youngest son, to join his brothers at Groton. Back in New York, she worked around the clock. She taught her classes at Todhunter in the morning. By noon she arrived at the headquarters for Governor Al Smith, Democratic candidate for president. There she organized the office, handled the mail, and

The Stock Market Crash

A company can sell shares of stock, which represent ownership in the company, to the public. If a company is successful, the demand for stock will increase along with the value of the stock. But, if a company is unsuccessful, the demand for the stock will decrease. In October 1929, many businesses started to fail. Panic set in and a record number of stocks were sold. Stock values dropped severely. Companies had to close and people lost their jobs. The period that followed the crash was marked by extreme poverty and became known as the Great Depression.

greeted visitors. It was often midnight before she returned home. Her closest friends were no longer those she had known as a debutante, but the teachers and activists with whom she worked.

Governor Smith wanted Franklin to replace him as governor; still Franklin was hesitant to run and refused to take Governor Smith's phone calls. Franklin worried that his health would not yet permit him to run a strong campaign. Sara was convinced the campaign would slow his recovery. But Eleanor finally persuaded him to take the call and Franklin agreed to accept the nomination.

The results of the 1928 election were unexpected. Governor Smith lost the presidency, but Franklin won the governorship. Once again, Eleanor would be moving her family to the capital in Albany.

Eleanor loved her work, her political activism, and her teaching, and did not want to give them up. Instead she broke with tradition: She took on the role of governor's wife, but she also continued her own work. Every Sunday evening she took the train to New York. She taught her classes on Mondays, Tuesdays, and Wednesdays, returning to Albany on Wednesday afternoon in time to receive guests for tea in the governor's mansion at 4:30 PM.

In Albany Eleanor looked after the governor's mansion, redecorating where she felt it was necessary. She had a swimming pool built for Franklin. She attended dinners and teas. She advised Franklin on his political appointments and encouraged him to choose women candidates. She gave interviews and wrote columns. Although she gave up her title of Editor, Eleanor continued to work on the *Women's Democratic News*. And she took care of her mail, dutifully answering every letter she received.

On October 29, 1929, the stock market collapsed, sending the U. S. economy into a tailspin. The construction of new homes came to a standstill. Unemployment increased drastically, and, by 1930, six million had lost their jobs. These people had no access to healthcare and little to eat.

During the Depression, unemployed men lined up outside soup kitchens in Chicago.

The stock market crash dramatically changed the role government would play in the everyday lives of citizens. The American people wanted their leaders to help them in their time of need. New Yorkers looked to Franklin to solve their problems. Franklin set up a state agency to offer relief, create jobs in public works and conservation, and provide food and clothing to those who had none.

Franklin was reelected governor for a second term in a landslide victory largely because of the help he provided New Yorkers. But his reelection was also due in no small part to Eleanor's popularity. Meanwhile, Louis Howe was plotting for Franklin to run for the presidency. Franklin believed that if he could help his home state of New York weather the economic depression, he could help the entire country as well.

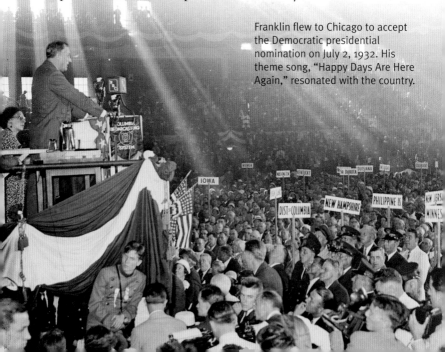

Franklin flew to Chicago to accept the Democratic presidential nomination on July 2, 1932. His theme song, "Happy Days Are Here Again," resonated with the country.

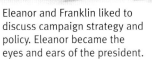

In 1932, Louis attended the Democratic presidential convention in Chicago while Eleanor and Franklin stayed at the governor's mansion in Albany. As the ballots were being cast, Eleanor sent out pots of coffee to the reporters who were gathered in the garage to hear the results. Later, while they waited, she worked on a sweater she was knitting for Louis. Once Franklin and Eleanor learned that Franklin had won the nomination, they did what no other candidate had ever done. Together with two of their children they boarded a plane to make a campaign appearance at the convention. They flew to Chicago, and there Franklin accepted the nomination in person, pledging to create a "new deal" for his country. He would restore America to greatness.

Eleanor and Franklin liked to discuss campaign strategy and policy. Eleanor became the eyes and ears of the president.

Franklin campaigned on a train known as the "Roosevelt Special" all the way across the country. The children took turns accompanying him. They helped him stand at rallies and made him laugh on the long journeys. Eleanor joined Franklin in Arizona for the return trip east. As they traveled they studied how people were coping with the Great Depression. They observed everything, from the cars people drove and the wash hanging on the clotheslines to the crops growing in the fields. Wherever they went, they sought ways the government could provide assistance.

chapter 12

The New Deal

On election night, November 8, 1932, Eleanor and Franklin gave a buffet supper for family and friends at their New York City townhouse, and then awaited the election results at the Biltmore Hotel. Eleanor greeted the campaign staff and supporters in the ballroom and also went to visit the Democratic state and national headquarters. When victory over Herbert Hoover was announced, the crowds went wild. Yet Eleanor remained surprisingly calm. She told reporters, many of whom were puzzled by her mood, that of course she was pleased but that she also recognized the enormity of the undertaking.

Eleanor worried about many of the changes she would have to make in her own life. She would no longer be able to do all the things she wanted to do. She liked teaching at Todhunter more than anything she had ever

Franklin promised a better future to Americans, especially to the many who were unemployed. Eleanor joined him on the "Roosevelt Special" and helped him win the election by seven million votes.

done, but now she would have to give it up. Although as the wife of the governor she had grown accustomed to a certain amount of scrutiny, she knew that as first lady she would be subject to even more. She dreaded the presence of the Secret Service and the lack of privacy for her and her family.

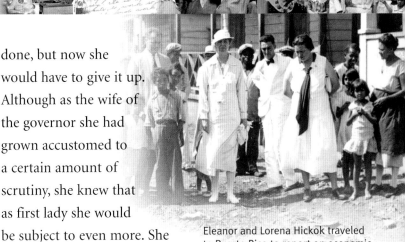

Eleanor and Lorena Hickok traveled to Puerto Rico to report on economic conditions during the Depression. Disheartened by the poverty, Eleanor was determined to help bring relief to the island.

One of the reporters who covered Eleanor Roosevelt, Lorena Hickok from the Associated Press, was quick to notice Eleanor's remarkable talents. She followed Eleanor closely and even wrote stories noting Eleanor's lack of enthusiasm on becoming first lady. As Lorena spent more time with Eleanor, the two became good friends. Eleanor could confide in Lorena and, in the weeks after the election, Lorena would help her through the transition process.

Franklin's inauguration took place on March 4, 1933, a cold and windy day. Eleanor wore a blue velvet dress and coat, a wide-brimmed hat, and white gloves. She carried a bouquet of orchids in her arms. After the swearing-in, Franklin assured the cheering crowds that "This great nation will endure as it has endured, will revive and will prosper." He vowed to provide jobs and warned that "The only thing

Eleanor and Franklin arrive at Union Station in Washington, D.C., on the eve of Franklin's first inauguration.

we have to fear is fear itself." Little did Eleanor know then the profound influence she, too, would have on her country. She was about to transform the role of first lady.

Still, for the first few months, Eleanor felt anxious and uneasy. She was not sure how she would fit in and what she would be able to accomplish. There was never any doubt of the difficulty of the task. Thirteen million Americans, more than a quarter of the nation, were unemployed. Banks had shut their doors.

But Eleanor was not one to remain idle. If her spirits were low, she would throw herself into her work. She continued to write articles and give radio speeches. She also wrote two books. In *It's Up to the Women!* Eleanor called on women to take action: "The women of today must have a vision of how to lead the world to peace." The other was a collection of her father's letters, *Hunting Big Game in the 'Eighties: The Letters of Elliott Roosevelt, Sportsman.* Here she attempted to explain why her father had left such a "vivid mark" not only on her, but on all those around him. "He loved people for the fineness that was in them and his friends might be newsboys or millionaires," she wrote.

Lorena Hickok suggested that Eleanor hold her own press conferences—something no other first lady had done. Eleanor embraced the idea and was soon holding regular press conferences in the White House for a group of 35 women reporters. Eleanor chose to include only women reporters to ensure that newspapers would both hire and keep women on staff.

Eleanor's daily routine never allowed for a free minute. She started most days with a horseback ride through Rock Creek Park, not far from the White House. After breakfast, Eleanor met with her housekeeper, Henrietta Nesbitt, and discussed the number of guests for meals.

Later in the morning Eleanor met with her assistant, Malvina Thompson, who had joined her from the governor's mansion in Albany. Tommy, as she was called, worked long hours and became devoted to Eleanor and her children. Together Eleanor and Tommy answered Eleanor's mail, which was no easy task. In her first

Eleanor answers reporters' questions, helping to pave the way for women journalists.

Eleanor discussed her schedule with Edith Helm, her social secretary, and her assistant, Malvina Thompson (Tommy).

year in the White House, Eleanor received 301,000 letters and replied to each one. She would either dictate a response or provide an outline for Tommy to complete.

Eleanor attended social functions in the afternoon and returned to her mail in the evening. She would sign the letters Tommy had prepared and also work on her articles and radio scripts. Every night, before retiring, she chose the most important papers, letters, or reports, and placed them in a basket which Franklin kept by his bedside. In the morning, Franklin would respond to the notes Eleanor had left behind.

If there were no formal functions planned, Eleanor sometimes escaped from the White House to go for outings with friends. She announced that she would drive her own car and refused to have a Secret Service agent accompany her. The head of the Secret Service protested, but Eleanor persisted. Finally, he approached Louis and told him that if Eleanor prevailed and drove her own car she would have to carry a revolver. Eleanor reluctantly accepted the revolver although she never intended to aim the gun at anyone.

Both Franklin and Eleanor looked for inventive ways to offer aid to the American people. They supported the establishment of several agencies to create jobs. The Civilian Conservation Corps put young men to work in national forests and parks. The Works Progress Administration gave jobs to artists, writers, actors, and musicians. Artists painted murals and writers wrote guidebooks to every state in the country. Eleanor took a special interest in the National Youth Administration, which offered jobs for as many as five million Americans, girls as well as boys. On August 14, 1935, Franklin signed the Social Security bill into law, providing retirement income for the elderly. Eleanor and Franklin had hoped that the benefits would be more extensive, but the law would prove to be only the beginning of a greater program that would later help the unemployed and the disabled.

In an effort to reach out to all Americans, Franklin gave informal talks, or what he called "fireside chats," on the radio. He wanted to reassure the nation and to offer hope for the "new deal" he had promised. Eleanor began to travel cross-country and to report on whatever conditions she

Eleanor carried a pistol so she could travel alone, unencumbered by the Secret Service.

MRS. ROOSEVELT CARRIES A PISTOL!

'Packs' a Weapon on Lone Auto Journeys---And Knows How to Use It

MRS. FRANKLIN D. ROOSEVELT AT WHEEL OF HER AUTOMOBILE
First Lady was Starting for a Drive Through Rock Creek Park.

found. Franklin expected her to be his "eyes and ears." Eleanor liked the adventure of travel and she was game to go anywhere.

In the autumn of 1933, Eleanor accompanied a group of Quakers to investigate conditions in the coal-mining area near Morgantown, West Virginia. What she found was appalling. For three years the men in the community had had little or no employment—most often working just one day a week. Children did not have much to eat. Eleanor said the food they ate looked like scraps one would give to a dog. There were no doctors to care for the children when they became sick. Strikes had led to violence, and many of the miners were living in tents.

Eleanor joined coal miners as they traveled down into a mine. Her visit drew attention to the miners' difficult lives.

Moved by what she saw, Eleanor helped establish a resettlement program to provide jobs for the miners. She took a special interest in one experimental housing development at Arthurdale, in West Virginia. Eleanor had been inspired by the work program she had started at Val-Kill and wanted to provide employment while creating

Newly constructed homes at Arthurdale, an experimental housing development in West Virginia, were well insulated and equipped with indoor plumbing.

a new community. With the help of Louis Howe, she raised public and private funds for men to build new homes on plots of between two and five acres. Women were trained in handcrafts such as quilt making and ceramics. Each family had a cow, a pig, and some chickens. They also grew their own vegetables.

Over the years, Eleanor devoted enormous energy and also provided substantial financial support to the project. Yet she was subject to criticism. Many Americans were outraged, opposing the large role government was playing. Nevertheless, Eleanor stayed involved. She insisted the money had been well spent. The miners and their families now had their own homes and their children attended school. The people had overcome their feeling of hopelessness and now had a sense of purpose.

chapter **13**

"The Trouble I've Seen"

In 1934, Louis Howe's health started to fail. He moved into the White House so that he could continue to consult the president. There he spent much of his time in bed, surrounded by newspapers. Both Franklin and Eleanor sought Louis's opinions and trusted his advice. When Louis died in April 1936, Franklin and Eleanor lost a true friend. James, their eldest son, moved to the White House to become Franklin's personal secretary and attempt to fill Louis's shoes. But the stress of the job proved so great that he soon had to resign.

That same year, Franklin ran for a second presidential term against Kansas governor Alfred M. Landon. This was Franklin's first campaign run without Louis, who had been behind Franklin in every campaign after his first election to the state senate in 1910. Still, Franklin won,

Eleanor installed slides, swings, and sandboxes on the White House lawn for her grandchildren. Here she is shown playing with Anna's children Sistie and Buzzie.

this time carrying every state except Maine and Vermont.

Eleanor returned to the White House more confident about what she could accomplish. Her work had become all consuming, yet as usual she found ways to mix family and work. The White House was always a whirlwind of activity. Both Franklin and Eleanor loved company,

Many Americans wore campaign buttons to support FDR.

and guests were almost always present. Eleanor often held three teas a week when she was in town, even though her feet, back, and shoulders would ache from shaking hands with so many people. The Roosevelts also entertained numerous overnight guests, including foreign officials. Several members of royalty stayed at the White House. One highlight was serving hot dogs to the King and Queen of England.

Lorena Hickok spent so much time at the White House that it felt like her home. She discovered she had become too close to Eleanor to cover her objectively and had resigned as an AP reporter. She was now working as a field reporter for Harry Hopkins, the director of the Works Progress Administration, who had become one of Franklin's closest advisers. Lorena wrote accounts of the poverty she found across the country—from the deep South to the tenements of Chicago, from the coal mines in Appalachia to California. All the children made frequent, and sometimes extended, visits to the White House. The older children, Anna, James, and Elliott, who were already married, came with their growing families. Eleanor set up nurseries on the third floor to accommodate the grandchildren. The younger sons, Franklin Jr. and John, were married during their father's second term, and they visited with their new brides.

Eleanor performed numerous official duties at Christmas time, but she relished the time with her family. On the morning of Christmas Eve, she presented Christmas stockings to children at a party at the National Theater. From there she went to the Salvation Army headquarters and then to Volunteers of America to distribute food baskets to the needy. Later, Eleanor and Franklin gave a party for the White House staff and their families

Eleanor and Franklin gathered all the family together for Christmas celebrations at the White House.

in the East Room, with its large tree beautifully decorated in white and silver. The entire family

THE ALLEYS

Many of Washington's poorest residents lived in shacks or old stables in the alleys behind some of the city's finer homes. The dilapidated housing had no indoor plumbing and was often rat-infested.

then attended the city tree-lighting ceremony near the White House, where Franklin broadcast a Christmas message to America. Afterward, Eleanor joined friends in singing carols in the Alleys, home to the city's least fortunate. Back at the White House, she found Franklin reading Charles Dickens's *A Christmas Carol* to the family. After the others went to bed, Eleanor filled the Christmas stockings and hung them in Franklin's room.

In the morning, the grandchildren came into "Papa's" room and climbed on his bed to open their stockings. The grown children, who also had stockings, laughed because Eleanor liked to include toothbrushes, soap, and nail files. After the stocking opening, Franklin had breakfast in bed and read the newspapers while the others went to church.

In the late afternoon, they gathered on the second floor to light the candles on the family tree, decorated by the older children. Then they opened the piles of presents that Eleanor had arranged on chairs around the room. The evening ended with a movie screening in the White House.

The first lady broke new ground by giving frequent radio addresses. The American public became familiar with her voice and came to know her intimately.

The next day Eleanor went back to work. At the age of 51, she signed a five-year contract with the United Feature Syndicate to write a column in the form of a diary. Called "My Day," it would appear in newspapers across the country six days a week. Eleanor never missed a deadline. If she knew she would have a particularly busy day or that she would be traveling, she would write and file her column in advance. After the 1936 election, "My Day" was appearing in 62 papers. Eleanor's column was straightforward and down-to-earth. Her style was casual and conversational. She wrote about issues that mattered most to her as well as about events in the news, the people she met, and her family life.

In the summer of 1936, Eleanor started to work on her autobiography. Her recollections of childhood were honest and sometimes painful. She found it more difficult to describe her adult years, not wanting to add detail that would hurt those she loved. The autobiography first appeared in the *Ladies' Home Journal* in serial form in 1937, and was then published by Harper & Brothers with the title *This Is My Story*. Eleanor dedicated the book "to the memory of my father who fired a child's imagination, and to the few other people who have meant the same inspiration throughout my life." The book's immediate success contributed to Eleanor's rising popularity.

Requests to give radio addresses or lectures multiplied. Eleanor was now paid one thousand dollars for each lecture, most of which went to the American Friends Service Committee to support the Arthurdale housing development. Eleanor took lessons to learn to project her voice and improve her elocution. She was even included on a designers' list of best dressed women, and it amused her to think how that would have surprised her older relatives.

Air travel allowed Eleanor to stick to her busy schedule. Once she and the famous aviator Amelia Earhart flew in evening dress from Washington, D.C., to Baltimore to promote air travel safety.

As Eleanor traveled across the country on lecture tours, she became increasingly aware of discrimination against African Americans. She argued

Americans around the country tuned into their radios to listen to the president's fireside chats and the first lady's talks.

Mary McLeod Bethune

Mary McLeod Bethune, the daughter of two former slaves, was born in South Carolina in 1875. She worked in cotton fields before attending a missionary school. She then taught school. In 1904, she established one of the first schools for African American girls in Florida, the Daytona Educational and Industrial School for Negro Girls (which later became Bethune-Cookman College). In 1935, Mary Bethune founded the National Council of Negro Women in Washington, D. C.

that the minimum wage should apply to African Americans as well as to white people. Disturbed that the residents of Arthurdale resisted integrating their community, she became determined to improve racial relations. Eleanor was most influenced by Mary McLeod Bethune, the African American women's and civil rights leader. The two first met at a dinner Eleanor hosted for national women leaders in 1927 and later became close friends. After Franklin was elected president, Mary McLeod Bethune was named a special adviser on racial affairs and, later, assistant director of the National Youth Administration.

Eleanor was repelled by the lynchings that still took place in the South. Mobs of white men would torture and kill African Americans accused of crimes. Eleanor fervently supported the anti-lynching bills put forth in Congress, as did her mother-in-law, Sara. Yet their efforts failed and the legislation did not pass.

LYNCH

To lynch is to put a person accused of a crime to death without due process of law or a fair trial.

In 1939, Howard University invited renowned African American singer Marian Anderson to give a concert in Washington. The university tried to reserve Constitution Hall, the largest auditorium in the city, for the performance. The Daughters of the American Revolution (DAR), an organization for the descendants of those who helped achieve American independence, refused to give the university permission, citing a "white performers only" policy. Eleanor chose to resign her membership in the DAR. An all-white high school in Washington, D.C., also turned Marian Anderson away. But the Department of the Interior, with Franklin's approval, granted permission for the concert to be held outdoors on the steps of the Lincoln Memorial. Marian Anderson sang on Easter Sunday in front of 75,000 people. She started with "America" and ended with the African-American spiritual "Oh, Nobody Knows the Trouble I've Seen."

Marian Anderson performed on the steps of the Lincoln Memorial.

14

World at War

By drawing attention to Marian Anderson, Eleanor succeeded in bringing the nation's attention to a terrible injustice. Meanwhile, Americans had become aware of battles on other fronts. Italy's fascist dictator Benito Mussolini had invaded Ethiopia. Japan had occupied Korea and Manchuria and invaded China. Adolf Hitler had risen to power and taken control of the German people. His Nazi party methodically arrested Jews and attacked their homes and synagogues. Hitler, driven by bigotry and greed, plotted to expand his territory. He annexed Czechoslovakia and, on September 1, 1939, invaded Poland. Two days later England and France declared war on Germany. Franklin had not planned to seek a third term. But, with the world in turmoil and

On July 18, 1940, Eleanor became the first woman to address a national political convention.

the threat of war imminent, he felt he had no choice. Eleanor also believed the people trusted Franklin. There was no other candidate strong enough to lead the country.

The president wanted Henry Wallace, Secretary of Agriculture, to be his running mate in the 1940 election, but several of Franklin's advisers thought he was too liberal to be a popular choice. Accompanied by her son Franklin, Eleanor flew to Chicago to stand in for her husband at the Democratic convention. She appeared in a blue dress, (her signature color, which was sometimes referred to as "Eleanor blue") and told the assembled delegates that the world faced "a grave and serious situation" and that the President would not campaign "in the usual sense of the word." She spoke simply and forcefully: "This is no ordinary time. No time for weighing anything except what we can best do for the country as a whole." Without mentioning the vice presidential candidates by name, she called for the people to unite behind their president. Henry Wallace won the vice-presidential nomination.

As the weeks passed, the war in Europe and fear at home intensified. The Netherlands and France had surrendered to Nazi Germany. Nazi bombers were attacking London and other parts of Britain. While Franklin made a campaign promise to keep American boys out of war, Eleanor hinted at another course. Always a strong peace advocate, she wanted to avoid war. But she was appalled by the news reports. She had begun to weigh the costs and benefits of remaining neutral. On November 2, 1940, Eleanor wrote in her column,

> "I kept praying that I might be able to prevent a repetition of the stupidity called war."
>
> Eleanor Roosevelt

"Today no one can honestly promise you peace at home or abroad. All any human being can do is promise that he will do his utmost to prevent this country from being involved in war."

Franklin defeated Wendell L. Wilkie, the Republican nominee, and made history by becoming the first president to win three terms. As the returns came in, Franklin and Eleanor greeted well-wishers on the front porch of Hyde Park. Those around Eleanor felt elated, but Eleanor focused on the pressure facing a war-time president.

Sir Winston Churchill, the British prime minister, urged Franklin to come to his country's aid in the war against the Nazis. Knowing Britain could not afford to buy American ships and weapons, Franklin asked Congress to pass the Lend-Lease Act to provide these materials on loan until the end of the war. In August 1941, Franklin told Eleanor he was going on a fishing trip. It was only a half-truth. Franklin traveled to Newfoundland, Canada, where he met secretly with Churchill aboard a warship. The two issued the Atlantic Charter, to declare common principles between the United States and Britain, including the establishment of safety and peace after the defeat of the Nazis. Although most of the country still wanted to

remain neutral, the bond between Franklin and Churchill would bring the United States closer to war.

The next few months would be especially difficult for Eleanor and Franklin. Missy LeHand, Franklin's longtime assistant, suffered a stroke so severe that it was impossible for her to work. In September 1941, Eleanor went to Hyde Park to see her mother-in-law, who had taken ill. Despite their differences, Eleanor had always been attentive to Sara's needs. When Eleanor saw Sara's condition she asked Franklin to come immediately. Franklin was with his mother when she died. Then, only a few weeks later, Eleanor's brother Hall died. To Eleanor it was like losing a child.

But there was little time to grieve as the demands on Eleanor's time multiplied. She took an active interest

All across Europe the Nazis arrested Jews, destroyed their homes, and sent them to concentration camps. Many of those imprisoned in the camps were killed in gas chambers.

Eva Peine and her parents fled to New York after Eva's father, a Jew, was released from the Sachsenhasuen concentration camp in Germany. In this letter Eva wrote Mrs. Roosevelt to ask for help in obtaining a job for her father.

in helping refugees, mainly European Jews who wanted to escape Hitler but could not obtain visas, official documents needed to enter the United States. Breckinridge Long, who was in charge of the government's visa division, had made the application process extremely difficult. He was unsympathetic to the plight of the Jews and disliked foreigners, especially Eastern Europeans. Eleanor did what she could to help the thousands of refugees, and she urged Franklin to help. Yet Franklin was sometimes reluctant to do as much as Eleanor asked. He knew that many Americans were unwilling to accept large numbers of new immigrants and he did not want to take an unpopular position.

In August 1940, the *S.S. Quanza*, a Portuguese freighter bearing Jewish refugees, docked in New York. It was one of the few refugee boats allowed into the U.S. at the time.

REFUGEES

Refugees leave their homelands to seek safety and protection in another country. They are often driven away by brutality and civil war, political and religious persecution, or severe economic conditions.

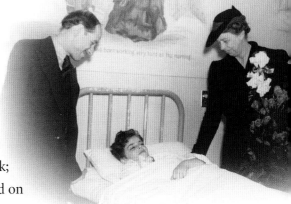

After word of Hitler's persecution of the Jews spread, Eleanor tried to help Jewish refugees. In February 1939, she visited the Jewish Hospital in Brooklyn.

Only those holding American visas were allowed to disembark; 83 refugees remained on board. The *Quanza* sailed to Mexico and there, too, the refugees were turned away. The ship made one more stop in Norfolk, Virginia, on her way back to Europe. Eleanor received an urgent plea to aid the refugees and persuaded Franklin to intervene. All the refugees on the *Quanza* were granted permission to enter the United States.

Office of Civilian Defense

In May 1941, Franklin established the Office of Civilian Defense (OCD) to protect the civilian population, maintain morale, and promote volunteer involvement in defense. Eleanor was put in charge of volunteer participation. Eleanor received undue criticism for her work, including her efforts to racially integrate the OCD. She resigned on February 20, 1942.

Eleanor also established the U. S. Committee for the Care of European Children. She saw to it that British refugee children not be treated as immigrants, but be issued visitor visas. She then convinced the State Department to agree to a president's advisory committee to review applications from political and intellectual refugees in

Japanese-American Internment Camps

After the bombing at Pearl Harbor, government officials regarded Japanese Americans as a threat to national security. They wanted to intern, or hold, them in camps. Eleanor considered these "internment camps" a violation of a citizen's basic rights. But on February 19, 1942, Franklin signed the order to intern thousands of Japanese Americans. In April 1943, he asked Eleanor to investigate camp conditions, which had sparked protests. On the basis of her report, Franklin began freeing interned Japanese Americans.

Spain, Portugal, and France.

But soon the nation would be pulled directly into the war. On December 7, 1941, the Japanese bombed Hawaii's Pearl Harbor. That day Eleanor told Americans: "We know what we have to face and we know that we are ready to face it." Franklin called December 7 a day "which will live in infamy" and he asked Congress to declare war. Congress then declared war on Japan and, on December 11, Germany and Italy declared war on the United States.

Sir Winston Churchill visited the White House over Christmas and returned again in June. Franklin and Churchill developed great affection for each other. Eleanor wrote, "It was a fortunate friendship. The war would have been harder to win without it."

While Eleanor's attention and concerns were with the war, she also worried about the backlash at home against Japanese Americans. In 1942, Franklin signed an order—which Eleanor strongly opposed—to move thousands of Japanese Americans from their homes to internment camps where many of them were held captive.

Later that year, Eleanor accepted Queen Elizabeth's invitation to visit American servicemen stationed in England and to see the wartime contributions of British women. She became the first wife of a president to go abroad without him, and the first to fly across the Atlantic.

Eleanor and her secretary, Tommy, stayed in Buckingham Palace where the royal family observed the same restrictions on heat, food, and water as commoners. A black line in Eleanor's bathtub indicated how much water she was allowed. King George and Queen Elizabeth showed them the king's rooms, damaged by bombs, and took them to St. Paul's Cathedral where they could look out across the city and view the devastation. They traveled outside London and visited country houses that had become nurseries for evacuated and wounded children.

As they traveled throughout London, Eleanor and Tommy saw how many homes had been damaged or destroyed by Nazi air raids.

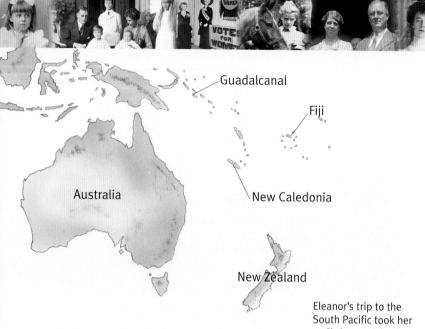

Guadalcanal

Fiji

Australia

New Caledonia

New Zealand

Eleanor's trip to the South Pacific took her to Christmas Island, New Caledonia, New Zealand, Fiji, Australia, and Guadalcanal.

Each day, despite the long hours, Eleanor wrote her column for the American newspapers assisted by Tommy.

All four Roosevelt boys joined the armed services. As she said good-bye to each of her sons, Eleanor thought it might be for the last time. She believed that "Life had to go on and you had to do what was required of you, but something inside of you quietly died." She knew mothers around the world shared the same feelings.

The women of New Zealand and Australia asked Eleanor to visit the South Pacific. Eleanor volunteered to go as a representative of the American Red Cross. In August 1943, she flew to Christmas Island and from there to New Caledonia, then on to New Zealand, Fiji, Australia, and Guadalcanal, covering a total of 25,000 miles (about 40,000 km). Everywhere she went she lifted spirits, visiting the wounded in hospitals,

This campaign button reflected the way many Americans felt about Franklin's accomplishments.

meeting and sharing meals with the troops. She was full of good cheer as she greeted 400,000 men in camps and hospitals. Yet in her heart she was overwhelmed by the destruction, the waste of human life, and a feeling of resentment that "men could not sit down around a table and settle their differences before an infinite number of the youth of many nations had to suffer."

In the spring of 1944, Franklin was running a low fever and the family became concerned about his health. Franklin asked his daughter, Anna, to assist him in the White House now that Missy was gone. Meanwhile Franklin prepared for the invasion of German-occupied France. On June 6, known as D-Day, 150,000 troops landed on the shores of Normandy in a surprise attack that would set in motion the liberation of Europe. In her "My Day" column, Eleanor wrote of the "long, hard fight" ahead and she called on all Americans to do everything in their power to hasten the end of the war.

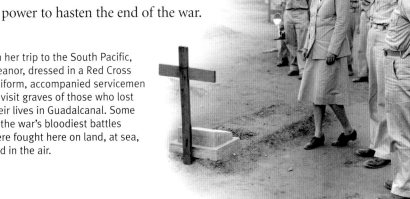

On her trip to the South Pacific, Eleanor, dressed in a Red Cross uniform, accompanied servicemen to visit graves of those who lost their lives in Guadalcanal. Some of the war's bloodiest battles were fought here on land, at sea, and in the air.

15

A New Calling

It came as no surprise to Eleanor that Franklin wanted to see the war through to the end. The country stood behind him, electing Franklin to a fourth term. Franklin summoned all 13 of the Roosevelt grandchildren to his inauguration on January 20, 1945. It was a simple ceremony, held this time on the south porch of the White House.

Two days later, Franklin, accompanied by his daughter, Anna, left for Yalta, a Soviet port on the Black Sea. There, he met secretly with Winston Churchill and Joseph Stalin, the leader of the Soviet Union. The three men made plans

Franklin's son James accompanied his father to the podium for the president's fourth—and last— inaugural address. Vice President Harry Truman stood to the far left.

to end the war and also discussed the founding of the United Nations, a new international organization to ensure peace. When Franklin returned to the United States weeks later, he had little energy. For the first time he did not stand to address Congress, but spoke from his wheelchair. Eleanor knew the stress of the war had taken its toll. Franklin was badly in need of rest. Accompanied by his two cousins, Laura Delano and Margaret Suckley, he left for Warm Springs.

On April 12, 1945, Eleanor was attending a charity event when she was called to the telephone. Press Secretary Steve Early asked her to return home immediately. The drive back to the White House was somber. Steve Early and Dr. Ross McIntire, the president's physician, waited for her in her sitting room. There they told her the president had died. Her husband had suffered a cerebral hemorrhage, which is bleeding in the brain.

The Soviet Union

Nicholas II, the last emperor and tsar of Russia, was overthrown in 1917. Civil war followed and resulted in the formation of the Soviet Union in 1922. It was composed of the territory that had once formed the Russian empire: Russia, Ukraine, Belorussia, and Transcaucasia. Its leaders, including Joseph Stalin, were Communists—people who believe that all property should be owned by the community as a whole and that all people should have equal economic status. The Communist Party in Moscow exercised political control over the entire country and limited people's basic rights, including freedom of speech. The Soviet Union fell in 1991, breaking into different countries.

Eleanor and her daughter, Anna, stood beside the coffin during the president's burial. Six black-draped horses had led the procession from the train station to the Rose Garden at Hyde Park. A hooded, riderless horse followed, symbol of the fallen leader.

Eleanor sent for Vice President Harry Truman to tell him what had happened. Her first thoughts were not of herself, but of the people of the country who had "lost their leader and friend before the war was really won." Later she would cable her sons, "He would expect you to carry on and finish your jobs." As soon as the new president was sworn in, Eleanor boarded the plane for Warm Springs.

Franklin's cousins were not the only guests at Warm Springs. Lucy Rutherford—the former Lucy Mercer whose love for Franklin had threatened his marriage many years before—was also present. In recent months Lucy, now widowed, had visited Franklin on occasion. They had renewed their friendship without becoming romantically involved, but they had kept their visits secret from Eleanor.

Eleanor discovered this only after she arrived in Warm Springs. She was deeply hurt but knew she must set an example for the country. She did her best to hide her resentment. The next morning, Eleanor, graceful and composed, accompanied Franklin's body on the train back to Washington. From the train window she watched the faces of the people who had gathered to pay tribute.

The funeral service in the East Room of the White House ended with the often-quoted words from Franklin's first inaugural address, "The only thing we have to fear is fear itself." Later the train carried Franklin's body to Hyde Park for burial in the Rose Garden. Once again, all through the night, Eleanor watched the crowds of people who had come out to pay their respects.

A child with polio stands in the Rose Garden at Hyde Park, where Franklin is buried. In the distance, Eleanor and others participate in a wreath-laying ceremony on the 77th anniversary of the president's birth.

Franklin died less than a month before Germany surrendered. With the end of the war came a tragic legacy. As Allied forces liberated Nazi concentration camps, the horrors of the Holocaust

The Holocaust

The Holocaust was the systematic persecution and killing of European Jews and others, including political prisoners, homosexuals, and the disabled, by Nazi Germany. Between 1933 and 1945, more than six million Jews were murdered.

were revealed. Then, on August 6, 1945, the atomic bomb, created secretly by American and British scientists, was dropped on Hiroshima, Japan, killing more than 140,000 people; three days later 70,000 people were killed at Nagasaki, Japan, by a second atomic bomb.

Eleanor, like Franklin, believed the United Nations was the one hope for a peaceful world. In December 1945, President Truman asked Eleanor to serve as a member of the U. S. delegation to the United Nations and to attend the first organizational meeting in London. Nothing could have pleased Eleanor more, but she doubted she had the background or experience she would need. Still, she wanted to support an organization that would promote peace by fostering cooperation between nations in areas of international law, security, and economic development. She accepted the nomination and the challenge.

As Eleanor crossed the ocean by boat on the *Queen Elizabeth* she read hundreds of documents that had been placed in her stateroom, many of them secret. Eleanor was assigned to work on a committee that dealt with humanitarian, educational, and cultural subjects. Once in London, she made an effort to meet the other women delegates, inviting them to tea in her sitting room at the hotel. Eleanor also arranged informal meetings with delegates of different nationalities, all of which helped her later to resolve conflicts and bring committee members together.

Still committed to helping war refugees, Eleanor skillfully negotiated a policy that would not force refugees to return to their homelands. She saw to it that many refugees who had fled from regions of Europe under Soviet control were not sent back against their will.

Eleanor was also named to the UN Human Rights Commission and was elected chair. She would consider the work she did for this commission her most important contribution in the six years she remained a UN delegate. The commission was given the task of writing an International Bill of Rights. This was a cause dear to Eleanor's heart. The document would define the most

Eleanor attended a meeting of the United Nations General Assembly with other U.S. delegates in September 1947.

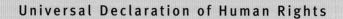

Universal Declaration of Human Rights

The Universal Declaration of Human Rights reaffirmed faith in the dignity of the human person and the equal rights of men and women. The Declaration began by assuring individual rights such as life, liberty, and personal security, bans on slavery and torture, and the right to fair criminal procedures. The document included the right to leave and return to a country and to seek political protection. Freedom of thought, religion, and peaceful assembly and association were also guaranteed. The Declaration ensured economic rights such as the right to receive equal pay for equal work or to join a trade union. Finally, the Declaration included the right to adequate food, housing, and medical care, the right to education, the right of parents to choose the kind of education for their children, and the right to participate in the cultural life of the community. Although the Declaration listed basic rights, it did not include the means to enforce them.

basic rights and include not only political and civil rights, but also social, economic, and cultural rights.

Members of the Commission included representatives from Lebanon, France, India, China, Canada, and the Soviet Union. Coming from countries with fundamental differences in their political and economic systems, they often disagreed about which rights should be included or which were most important. One of Eleanor's great skills was that she could work well with a diverse group of people. She was practiced at building consensus.

The Commission met in New York, Geneva, and Paris to agree on general principles as well as specific wording.

Eleanor insisted the members work long hours. By September 1948, they had completed a draft of the Universal Declaration of Human Rights. They then debated every word of the draft before its final revisions were approved. On December 10, 1948, the UN General Assembly formally accepted the Declaration. Once the votes were cast, the entire assembly of delegates rose to give Eleanor a standing ovation. For the first time in history, representatives of different nations had come together to declare basic rights and freedoms that should be enjoyed by all peoples.

Eleanor's sheer force of personality had contributed greatly to the successful outcome. In meeting after meeting Eleanor had exhibited her warmth, charm, and humor. She was also doggedly persistent.

Eleanor believed that "The Human Rights Commission was one of the important parts of the foundation on which the United Nations might build a peaceful world."

16

Life as an Adventure

Eleanor continued to serve as U. S. delegate to the United Nations until 1952, when General Dwight D. Eisenhower won the presidential election. Eleanor then resigned from her post as it was expected that President Eisenhower, a Republican, would choose his own representatives. Eleanor had never been one to seek recognition for the work she did, yet she received well-earned praise for her contribution and her six years of service. Nineteen newly formed African countries would make references to the provisions of the Universal Declaration of Human Rights in their new constitutions.

Although her official appointment had ended, Eleanor still remained engaged in international affairs. In fact, she became more determined than ever to

Eleanor traveled for a month in India, and met with people from all walks of life, including Jawaharlal Nehru, prime minister of the newly independent country (to the left of Eleanor).

see parts of the world where she had never been. And, since she was still a newspaper woman writing a daily column, she had a ready-made audience for her observations and commentary. After ending her appointment at the United Nations General Assembly in Paris, Eleanor did not return home right away, but set off to see the world.

Eleanor flew first to the Middle East, stopping in Lebanon, Syria, Jordan, and Israel. Her visit resulted in mixed emotions. The hundreds of thousands of Jewish refugees from Europe who had settled in Israel were leading productive lives. However, the Palestinian refugees who had been forced to leave Israeli territory lived in camps under appalling conditions. Eleanor was equally distressed when, later on her journey, she visited Pakistan and India and realized how disputes between these neighboring peoples led to vast expenditures of money on defense, money that would be better spent on health, housing, and education.

Meeting Prime Minister Jawaharlal

The Taj Mahal

The Taj Mahal in Agra, India, is considered one of the most beautiful buildings in the world. It was built in the 17th century of white marble by the emperor Shah Jehan to house his wife's tomb as well as his own.

Nehru of India and other officials, Eleanor was impressed with the leaders' "passionate devotion" to democracy. She thought many Americans now took so many of their freedoms for granted. She wrote, "Perhaps we may draw from people who ford rivers and walk miles of jungle trails in order to vote a new sense of our responsibility." She concluded that the people of India were well aware of the material values of Americans, but knew little of their spiritual values. Americans needed to show by their behavior the importance they gave to equality, justice, and charity.

Eleanor also visited the Taj Mahal, where she recalled her father's Indian adventures. He had once promised to take her to see the Taj Mahal, but he had died too soon. Now she was moved by its beauty and happy for the memory she would always carry with her. Later she would publish an account of her travels in her book *India and the Awakening East*.

Over the next few years, Eleanor received many invitations to visit other countries. Her curiosity, her sincere interest in other people, and her goodwill were readily apparent. She was admired wherever she went and soon earned the title "First Lady of the World."

In the spring of 1953, Eleanor was asked to participate in an exchange program in Japan and to discuss the role of women in a democracy. She talked to Empress Nagako about the changing lives of women. She also interviewed Emperor Hirohito, who expressed an interest in Japan joining the United Nations. While visiting a home for orphans at Hiroshima, Eleanor wished with her whole heart "that men could learn from this that we know too well how to destroy and must learn instead how to prevent such destruction." As she witnessed the suffering she felt more strongly than ever that it was only possible to eliminate the causes of war by using "the machinery of the United Nations."

Eleanor spent five weeks in Japan in the spring of 1953. She traveled to Hiroshima, where the U.S. dropped the first atomic bomb, on August 6, 1945.

A Muslim leader spent time with Eleanor in Tashkent, a city in central Asia.

The more Eleanor traveled, the more she realized how important it was to be open to other cultures. She toured Bali in the South Sea, Jakarta in Indonesia, Bangkok in Thailand, and Morocco in North Africa. In 1957, Dorothy Schiff, the publisher of the *New York Post*, asked Eleanor to write a series of articles on the Soviet Union. After World War II, the Soviet Union had expanded both its economy and its influence. By spreading communism into Eastern Europe and other parts of the world, the Soviets had alienated their former allies, the United States and the United Kingdom. Accompanied by Maureen Corr, her secretary, and David Gurewitsch, her physician and good friend, she spent a month traveling across the Soviet Union. David, who was the son of Russian Jews, acted as her interpreter. They visited government officials in Moscow, farms in Tashkent, historical relics in Samarkand (one of the oldest cities in the world), and a medical school in Leningrad, now St. Petersburg.

It was not until three days before her departure that Nikita S. Khrushchev, the Soviet leader and once one of Stalin's top advisers, consented to an interview.

They discussed disarmament and communism but found little common ground. Only on one issue could they agree: They both believed that in order to reduce misunderstandings and fear they needed to promote a broader exchange of people and ideas. Eleanor returned home even more determined to reach out to people of different cultures.

Eleanor wanted young Americans to live and work among people of other religions and colors so that they could learn from each other. "We must provide leadership for free peoples," she wrote. "But we must never forget that in many countries, particularly in Asia and Africa, the freedom that is uppermost in the minds of the people is freedom to eat."

Warning young people not to choose security over adventure, she offered this advice: "Do not stop thinking of life as an adventure. You have no security unless you can live bravely, excitingly, imaginatively."

In 1959, two years after Eleanor's trip to the Soviet Union, Nikita Khrushchev and his wife Nina visited Eleanor at Hyde Park.

chapter 17

"You Learn by Living"

Back at home, Eleanor wrote her column, gave lectures, and stayed active in world affairs. Twice a week, she volunteered for the American Association for the United Nations, an educational organization that promotes the goals of the UN. She was a successful fundraiser for the National Foundation for Infantile Paralysis, the National Association for the Advancement of Colored People (NAACP), and the Citizens' Committee for Children, a group that spoke for New York City children, especially those born into poverty. Eleanor always remained open to new experiences. "Life was meant to be lived, and curiosity must be kept alive," she once wrote. "One must never, for whatever reason, turn his back on life."

Eleanor divided her time between New York and Val-Kill. In the end, the furniture business Eleanor had started with her friends had not proved profitable.

Fala, a Scottish terrier, was Franklin's faithful companion. After Franklin's death, Eleanor grew increasingly attached to Fala. In April 1952, Fala died and was buried in the Rose Garden at Hyde Park.

As first lady, Eleanor had had little time to oversee it, so she had closed the factory at Val-Kill. She had then converted the building into her own home. The wood paneling and the dozens of photographs lining the walls gave the house a cozy feeling. Eleanor often wrote her "My Day" column from the upstairs sleeping porch overlooking the pond.

Family and friends visited often and enjoyed the woods, the wildflowers, and the pool. Eleanor entertained world leaders here, including Nikita and Nina Khrushchev, President Tito of Yugoslavia, Prime Minister Nehru of India, and Emperor Haile Selassie from Ethiopia.

As Eleanor grew older, she remembered mostly the happy times she had shared with Franklin. Over the years, the memories of any unhappiness between them faded and she thought of Franklin fondly. She recognized how much he had done for the country and she was proud to have shared in his achievements. At the same time, she was glad she had never hesitated to leave her own mark.

Sunrise at Campobello

The play *Sunrise at Campobello* opened in 1958 on January 30, Franklin's birthday. It starred Ralph Bellamy as Franklin and soon became a Broadway hit. Written and produced by Dore Schary, it told the story of the summer of 1921 when Franklin contracted polio at Campobello and struggled to overcome his illness. The play dealt with personal issues and private lives and painted Franklin's mother in an unfavorable light. Yet it also underscored Franklin and Eleanor's tremendous spirit and courage.

Eleanor kept up many of their family traditions. At Fourth of July picnics, Eleanor or one of her children would read the Declaration of Independence and the Bill of Rights.

On Christmas morning Eleanor would leave a stocking stuffed with candy, nuts, and trinkets outside each bedroom door. Her grandchildren liked to give her huge baskets filled with painted pine cones, which they then burned in the fireplace, watching the flames turn colors. Her Christmas toast was the same Franklin had given for many years, "To the United States of America." Eleanor always added, "And to those we love who are not with us today." After dinner, Eleanor showered presents on her family and friends. And before turning in, she would read aloud from *A Christmas Carol*, just as Franklin had done when he was alive.

Wherever she was, Eleanor always surrounded herself with her friends. As she loved to entertain, guests were always welcome for dinner. (The housekeeper considered 12 a small number.) Eleanor never forgot a friend's birthday and remained loyal to the many friends she had known over the years. Many dear friends spent Thanksgiving and Christmas with Eleanor and her family at Val-Kill. They included Lorena Hickok, who had moved to an apartment in the village of Hyde Park; her confidant David Gurewitsch and his wife, Edna; and Joe Lash (the United Nations correspondent for the *New York Post*) and his wife, Trude.

April of 1953 brought the death of one of Eleanor's closest friends, "Tommy" Thompson. She had been Eleanor's assistant for 25 years and the two had traveled hundreds of thousands of miles together. She was devoted to the Roosevelt children and grandchildren and had become almost a member of the family. Eleanor would

Eleanor kept this picture of Joe Lash in her wallet. They first met when she was first lady and he was a young man active in social reform. He would later write a Pulitzer-Prize winning biography of Eleanor.

Eleanor enjoyed talking to the boys from Wiltwyck School at the annual picnic she hosted.

always treasure a birthday card on which Tommy had written, "It makes me very happy to feel that to some degree I am necessary to you."

Eleanor also showed a great interest in the troubled youth at the Wiltwyck School for Boys, located across the Hudson River from Hyde Park. She had worked hard to help the school, serving on its board of directors and raising badly needed funds. She donated furniture to the school office and often contributed her lecture fees to the school. Every summer Eleanor, with help from her grandchildren, would hold a picnic for

"Above all, you have kept love alive in a generation sick with hatred."

Archibald MacLeish,
former Librarian of Congress

the boys from Wiltwyck School. Close to 150 boys would arrive by bus to spend the afternoon at Hyde Park, enjoying hot dogs, beans, corn on the cob, and coleslaw, as well as cupcakes and ice cream for dessert. Eleanor read aloud to them from the classic *Just So Stories* by Rudyard Kipling.

The boys' choir at Wiltwyck School paid a surprise visit to Eleanor on October 11, 1954, Eleanor's 70th birthday. They presented her with a gift of one hundred handmade potholders and sang her favorite song, "Beautiful Dreamer." They performed again that night at the Waldorf-Astoria Hotel in New York City, the same grand hotel where, at the age of 18, Eleanor had made her society debut. That night the ball had been "utter agony." This time one thousand guests were gathered in her honor. The party was to be a fund-raiser for the American Association for the United Nations. Tributes, letters, and telegrams had poured in from all across the world, from singer Marian Anderson and poet Langston Hughes, from Queen Elizabeth of England,

Eleanor's 70th birthday cake was decorated with flags from around the world and topped with a globe.

Herbert Block, called Herblock, the editorial cartoonist, presented Eleanor with this drawing for her 70th birthday. It hung on the wall of her home in Val-Kill.

Princess Wilhelmina of the Netherlands, and Prime Minister Nehru of India, from Albert Einstein and Helen Keller.

A telegram from Channing H. Tobias, the NAACP chair, included these words: "Your steadfast courage has inspired others to stand firm against all forms of bigotry." Mary McLeod Bethune wrote, "I bless you for the ways in which you have made my efforts easier and my tasks more productive.... You are a citizen of the world.... Men and women in all parts of the world have been inspired by you to lift their heads, stand firmly upon their feet and take a stand for human values." Author Pearl S. Buck wrote, "Not the least of my pride in all that you have done and are is that you are a woman and have never let womanhood be a handicap."

Eleanor once again became involved in politics, this time campaigning for Adlai Stevenson, the Democratic candidate in the 1956 presidential race. She kept a hectic schedule, sometimes racing from one city to another so she could keep two speaking engagements in the same evening. She also traveled once a week to Brandeis University in Boston

to teach a course in international law and organization. She
hosted an interview program on Boston public television,
sponsored by Brandeis. Each day was so full that she had
to stay up well past midnight to answer her mail. Eleanor's
children urged her to slow down, but she refused.

Eleanor loved being a grandmother and her 22
grandchildren adored her.
As busy as she was with work,

Eleanor and her grandchildren,
Nina (center) and Sally, walked
Fala around Hyde Park.

she put them all at ease and made each one feel special. She read stories to the young ones and took the older children on trips. In 1959, she traveled with her granddaughter Nina (her son John's child) to Israel and Iran. Nina was touched by the gentle and caring way Eleanor spoke to the people she met in hospitals or tin shacks. Eleanor shared her deep faith in the United Nations with her daughter's son John, who became involved in the American Association for the United Nations during his years at Amherst College. When John graduated in 1960, Eleanor spoke at the commencement.

John F. Kennedy

In the 1960 presidential race, Eleanor supported Adlai Stevenson for the Democratic nomination, claiming he had greater maturity and experience than John F. Kennedy, the young senator from Massachusetts. After Kennedy won the nomination, he sought Eleanor's support and visited her at Val-Kill on August 10, 1960. Impressed with Kennedy's "quick mind," she agreed to campaign for him. Eleanor found he was "a likable man with charm" and "hospitable to new ideas." Kennedy won the election against Richard Nixon by a slim margin.

That same year, John F. Kennedy, the Democratic senator from Massachusetts, was elected president. He asked Eleanor to serve as a delegate to the United Nations, as well as on the Advisory Commission to the Peace Corps. President Kennedy had started this new program to send young volunteers out into the world to serve the cause of peace by working in developing countries. Eleanor also chaired the President's Commission on the Status of Women, promoting equal pay for equal work and better education for women.

Eleanor wrote several books, including the second volume of her autobiography, *This I Remember*, chronicling the years 1921-1945, and the last volume, *On My Own*, published in 1958. In her book *You Learn by Living*, published in 1960, Eleanor discussed the importance of learning to be useful and making the most of every experience. She

John's daughter Nina enjoyed long walks and picnics with her grandmother and later accompanied her on her world travels.

wrote of the wisdom in those who have the courage "to stand up and be counted, even when it makes one unpopular." Eleanor was always open to new ideas and willing to work for change. It was this remarkable strength that made her granddaughter Nina Gibson say, "I never thought of her as old in the slightest."

chapter 18

Her Glow Warms the World

By the summer of 1962, Eleanor's health was deteriorating and she could not keep the busy schedule to which she had grown accustomed. One day, she brought a picnic to Tivoli, the home where she had been raised by her grandmother, aunts, and uncles. It would be for the last time. She also returned to Campobello Island where she had spent many summers with her family and where Franklin had become ill with polio. On this occasion Eleanor was so weak it was hard for her to walk to her favorite places on the island. In her "My Day" column she recalled "the deep mossy paths," "the dark mysterious woods," and "the beautiful sunsets."

Anna Eleanor Roosevelt holds her five-week-old namesake, Maria Anna, the daughter of her close friends David and Edna Gurewitsch.

"Every corner had its memories," her devoted friend and doctor, David Gurewitsch, who accompanied her

to Campobello, wrote. "Though she never put it into words, here she was going back in time."

In September, Eleanor entered the hospital, where David and other doctors determined that she had a rare form of tuberculosis. She spent her 78th birthday in the hospital, and shortly thereafter returned home. Her family gathered in New York to be with her. David and his wife, Edna, checked on her daily. David did everything he could to save her, but on November 7, 1962, Eleanor died.

Eleanor was buried in the Rose Garden at Hyde Park next to her husband. Close friends, as well as presidents and world leaders, joined the family for the service. Those in attendance included President Kennedy and his wife, Jacqueline; Vice-President Lyndon Johnson and his wife, Lady Byrd; former President Dwight D. Eisenhower; former President Harry Truman, his wife, Bess and his daughter, Margaret; and U Thant, the Secretary General of the United Nations.

In a eulogy at the United Nations on November 9, Adlai Stevenson, U.S. Ambassador to the UN, said of Eleanor, "For she would rather light candles than curse the darkness, and her glow had warmed the world." He spoke again of his good and fearless friend on November 17 at the Cathedral of

President Kennedy and the first lady attended graveside services for Eleanor at Hyde Park. Standing to the right of the President are Vice President Lyndon B. Johnson, former President Harry S. Truman and his wife, Bess, and former President Dwight D. Eisenhower.

St. John the Divine where 10,000 people gathered for a memorial service.

As a small child, Eleanor had had little confidence in herself. Many in her family had called her an "ugly duckling" and thought she would not amount to much. But she led a rich life, surpassing everyone's expectations—including her own.

As a much-loved teacher, a prolific writer, and a political activist, she worked to combat discrimination and to improve the lives of the less fortunate.

As first lady, she formed an unprecedented partnership with her husband. Eleanor's influence over Franklin was

extraordinary. She spoke her mind and helped Franklin to see the world in new ways.

As a U.S. delegate to the United Nations and as a world traveler, she worked to make a more peaceful world. She considered the Universal Declaration of Human Rights to be her greatest achievement. It is a document that will endure through the ages to assure greater equality and justice for all.

Eleanor was able to achieve all this in large part because she grew to believe that she could. In her book *You Learn by Living*, she wrote, "Surely, in the light of history, it is more intelligent to hope rather than to fear; to try rather than to not try. For one thing we know beyond all doubt: Nothing has ever been achieved by the person who says, 'It can't be done.'"

Visitors pay tribute to Eleanor at the Franklin Delano Roosevelt Memorial in Washington, D.C. Throughout her life Eleanor worked to make a more peaceful world; she left it a better place.

Events in the Life of Eleanor Roosevelt

October 11, 1884
Eleanor Roosevelt ("Little Nell") is born in New York City.

September 14, 1901
Theodore Roosevelt, Eleanor's uncle, becomes president of the United States following the assassination of William McKinley.

Autumn 1903
Eleanor teaches classes at the Rivington Street Settlement House in the Lower East Side of Manhattan.

March 17, 1905
Eleanor marries her distant cousin Franklin Delano Roosevelt.

August 1921
While on vacation with his family at Campobello Island, Franklin is struck by polio. His legs remain paralyzed.

1926
Together with her friends Nancy Cook and Marion Dickerman, Eleanor starts Val-Kill Industries, a furniture-making business near the Roosevelt estate at Hyde Park.

September 1899
Eleanor enrolls at Allenswood, an English boarding school outside London.

May 3, 1906
Anna Eleanor Roosevelt, the first of Eleanor and Franklin's six children, is born.

April 16, 1917
The United States enters World War I. Eleanor volunteers at the Red Cross canteen and in naval hospitals in Washington, D.C.

1928
Franklin's election as governor makes Eleanor first lady of New York. She continues to teach at Todhunter School for Girls in New York.

1922
Eleanor joins the Women's Trade Union League, beginning a long career of political activism.

October 29, 1929
The U.S. stock market crashes marking the beginning of the Great Depression.

August 1943
Eleanor visits U.S. soldiers stationed in the South Pacific.

December 10, 1948
The United Nations formally accepts the Universal Declaration of Human Rights. Eleanor considered this her greatest achievement.

1937
This Is My Story, the first volume of Eleanor's autobiography, receives critical acclaim.

March 6, 1933
Eleanor holds the first of her weekly press conferences for women reporters.

April 12, 1945
Franklin dies of a cerebral hemorrhage in Warm Springs, Georgia.

December 30, 1935
Eleanor's newspaper column, "My Day," appears for the first time in newspapers around the country.

1945-1952
Eleanor serves as U.S. delegate to the United Nations, chairing the UN Human Rights Commission for two of these years.

December 7, 1941
The U. S. enters World War II after the Japanese make a surprise attack on Pearl Harbor.

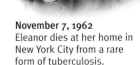

March 4, 1933
Eleanor becomes first lady as Franklin is sworn in as president of the United States. He would serve as president for an unprecedented four terms. Eleanor influenced FDR greatly during his time in office.

November 7, 1962
Eleanor dies at her home in New York City from a rare form of tuberculosis.

Bibliography

Black, Allida M. *Casting Her Own Shadow: Eleanor Roosevelt and the Shaping of Postwar Liberalism*. New York: Columbia University Press, 1996.

---, ed. *Courage in a Dangerous World: The Political Writings of Eleanor Roosevelt*. New York: Columbia University Press, 1999.

Cook, Blanche Wiesen. *Eleanor Roosevelt*. Volumes 1 & 2. New York: Viking Penguin, 1992 & 1999.

The Eleanor Roosevelt Encyclopedia, edited by Maurine H. Beasley, Holly C. Shulman, and Henry R. Beasley. Westport, Connecticut: Greenwood Press, 2001.

Eleanor Roosevelt's My Day: Her Acclaimed Columns. Volumes I, II, III. New York: Pharos Books, 1989-1991.

Freedman, Russell. *Eleanor Roosevelt; A Life of Discovery*. New York: Clarion Books, 1993.

Gibson, Nina Roosevelt. Interview by Emily Williams, oral historian, 13 Aug. 1979, for Franklin D. Roosevelt Library.

Glendon, Mary Ann. *A World Made New: Eleanor Roosevelt and the Universal Declaration of Human Rights*. New York: Random House, 2001.

Goodwin, Doris Kearns. *No Ordinary Time; Franklin and Eleanor Roosevelt: The Home Front in World War II*. New York: Simon & Schuster, 1994.

Gurewitsch, A. David, M. D. *Eleanor Roosevelt: Her Day*. New York: Quadrangle/The New York Times Co., 1974.

Gurewitsch, Edna P. *Kindred Souls: The Devoted Friendship of Eleanor Roosevelt and Dr. David Gurewitsch*. New York: St. Martin's Press, 2002.

Harrity, Richard, & Ralph G. Martin. *Eleanor Roosevelt: Her Life in Pictures*. New York: Duell, Sloan & Pearce, 1958.

Johnson, Walter, ed. *The Papers of Adlai E. Stevenson*. Volume 8. Boston: Little, Brown, 1979.

Lash, Joseph P. *Eleanor and Franklin: The Story of Their Relationship, Based on Eleanor Roosevelt's Private Papers*. New York: W. W. Norton & Co., 1971.

---. *Eleanor: The Years Alone*. New York: W. W. Norton & Co., 1972.

MacLeish, Archibald. *The Eleanor Roosevelt Story*. Boston: Houghton Mifflin Company, 1965.

Meacham, Jon. *Franklin and Winston: An Intimate Portrait of an Epic Friendship*. New York: Random House, 2003.

Mother & Daughter: The Letters of Eleanor Anna Roosevelt, edited by Bernard Asbell. New York: Coward, McCann & Geoghegan, 1982.

Pottker, Jan. *Sara and Eleanor: The Story of Sara Delano Roosevelt and Her Daughter-in-Law, Eleanor Roosevelt*. New York: St. Martin's Press, 2004.

Purcell, Sarah J., & L. Edward. *The Life and Work of Eleanor Roosevelt*. Indianapolis: Alpha Books, 2002.

Roosevelt, Anna Eleanor, ed. *Hunting Big Game in the Eighties: The Letters of Elliott Roosevelt Sportsman*. New York: Charles Scribner's Sons, 1933.

Roosevelt, David, with Manuela Dunn Mascetti. *Grandmere: A Personal History of Eleanor Roosevelt*. New York: Warner Books, 2002.

Roosevelt, Eleanor. *The Autobiography of Eleanor Roosevelt*. New York: Da Capo Press, 1992.

---. *Eleanor Roosevelt's Christmas Book*. New York: Dodd, Mead, 1963.

---. *India and the Awakening East*. New York: Harper & Brothers, Publishers, 1953.

---. *It's Up to the Women*. New York: Frederick A. Stokes Co., 1933.

---. *On My Own*. New York: Harper & Brothers Publishers, 1958.

---. *You Learn by Living*. Louisville: Westminster John Knox Press, 1960.

---. *This Is My Story*. New York: Harper & Brothers, 1937.

Roosevelt, Elliott and James Brough. *Mother R: Eleanor Roosevelt's Untold Story*. New York: Putnam, 1977.

---. *An Untold Story; the Roosevelts of Hyde Park*. New York: G. P. Putnam's Sons, 1973

Schary, Dore. *Sunrise at Campobello; a play in three acts*. Dramatists Play Service Inc., 1957.

Seagraves, Eleanor. Interview by Dr. Thomas F. Soapes, oral historian, 2 Feb. 1978, for Franklin D. Roosevelt Library.

Springwood (photography by Richard Creek; text by Franklin D. Mares). Roosevelt-Vanderbilt Historical Association and Fort Church Publishers, 1993.

Works Cited

10: "one of the most brilliant" *New York Times*. 2 Dec. 1883. p. 3.

11: "miracle from heaven" *The Autobiography of Eleanor Roosevelt*, p. 5.

11: "She is such a funny child..." *Autobiography*, p. 9.

17: "I am thinking of you always..." *Hunting Big Game in the Eighties*, p. 168.

20: "In a month..." *Hunting Big Game*, p. 178.

28: "I really marvel..." *Autobiography*, p. 25.

31: "had the most admirable influence... Eleanor's report card, FDR library.

33: "You would have known..." letter from Marie Souvestre, FDR library.

37: "Unless you can swear..." Lash, *Eleanor and Franklin*, p. 108.

39-40: "Dearest mama..." MacLeish, p. 19.

41: "I am as fond..." letter from Theodore Roosevelt, FDR library.

44: "I was beginning to be..." *Autobiography*, p. 55.

58: "Have something you want to say..." *Autobiography*, p 124.

70: "The women of today..." *It's Up to the Women*, p. 239.

70-71: "He loved people..." *Hunting Big Game in the Eighties*, p. 157.

85: "This is no ordinary time..." *New York Times*, 19 July 1940. p. 5.

86: "I kept praying..." *Autobiography*, p. 251.

90: "We know what we have to face..." weekly radio address, www.gwu.edu/~erpapers/abouteleanor/q-and-a/q21-pearl-harbor-address.htm

91: "It was a fortunate friendship..." *Autobiography*, p. 237.

92: "Life had to go on..." *Autobiography*, p. 251.

93: "men could not sit down..." *Autobiography*, p. 261.

93: "long, hard fight." 7 June 1944. *Eleanor Roosevelt's My Day*. Vol. I, p. 342.

96: "to have lost their leader..." and "He would expect you..." *Autobiography*, p. 276.

101: "the Human Rights Commission..." *Autobiography*, p. 322.

104: "passionate devotion" and "Perhaps we may draw..." *Autobiography*, p. 330.

105: "that men could learn..." *Autobiography*, p. 340.

105: "machinery of the United Nations." *Autobiography*, p. 341.

107: "We must provide leadership..."*Autobiography*, p. 384.

107: "Do not stop thinking..." *Autobiography*, p. 409.

108: "Life was meant..." *Autobiography*, p. xix.

110: "To the United States..." Elliott Roosevelt, *Mother R.*, p. 86.

112: "It makes me..." Undated letter from Malvina Thompson, FDR library.

112-114: "Above all..." and all 70th birthday tributes, FDR library.

113: "utter agony." *Autobiography*, p. 37.

116: "quick mind..." 17 Aug. 1960...." *Eleanor Roosevelt's My Day*. Vol. III, pp. 252-253.

117: "to stand up and be counted..." *You Learn by Living*, p. 186.

117: "I never thought..." Gibson, p. 100.

118-119: "deep mossy paths..."10 Aug. 1962. *Eleanor Roosevelt's My Day*. Vol. III, p. 314.

119: "Every corner..." Edna Gurewitsch, p. 272.

120: "For she would rather..." Johnson, p. 339.

121: "Surely, in the light of history..." *You Learn by Living*, p. 168.

Index

Bethune, Mary McLeod 82, 114

Churchill, Sir Winston 86–87, 94–95

Grandmother Hall 6–7, 17, 18–25, 30, 32

Great Depression 64, 65–66, 67, 69–70, 73–75

Howe, Louis 47–48, 55, 57–58, 66, 75, 76

human rights 99–101, 102, 107, 121

labor issues 37, 57–58, 61, 74–75

Nazis and Adolf Hitler 84, 85, 86, 87, 88, 97

Nehru, P. M. Jawaharlal 103–104, 109, 114

philanthropy 8–9, 12, 17, 21, 35–36, 70–71

polio 54–55, 59–60, 97, 109

Pussie (aunt) 19, 21, 23–24, 30, 32–33

racial persecution 82, 83, 90

radio and television 73, 80, 81, 115

refugees 88, 89–90, 92, 99

religious persecution 84, 87, 88–89, 97–98, 103

Roosevelt, Anna (daughter) 44, 49, 53, 57, 59, 78, 93

Roosevelt, Anna Eleanor "Eleanor"

legacy 6–7, 119–121

life 122–123

childhood and adolescence 6–7, 11, 12–25, 28–31

early adulthood 32–37

courtship and wedding 34–35, 37, 39–40, 41–43

birth of children 44–45, 46, 49

as a teacher 62–63, 65, 68

as First Lady 69, 70–74, 77, 78–79, 120–121

at husband's death 95–96

later years 108–117

death 119–120

political activities, personal campaigns 63–64, 114

children's issues 21, 35–36, 61, 73, 90, 108, 112–113

civil rights 81–83, 108

housing 75, 81

human rights 99–101, 102, 107, 121

labor issues 60–61, 74–75

refugee aid 88, 89, 90, 99, 103

for the U. N. 98–101, 102, 105, 108, 113

women's issues 36–37, 53, 57–58, 70, 71, 82, 105

political activities for Franklin 47–49, 56, 65, 67–70, 72, 74, 85

Roosevelt, Anna Hall (mother) 6, 10, 11, 12, 14–16, 17

Roosevelt, Elliott (father) 6, 9–14, 16–17, 19–21, 22, 34

Roosevelt, Elliott (son) 46, 48, 53, 78, 92

Roosevelt, Elliott, Jr. (brother) 13, 17, 18–19

Roosevelt, Franklin, Jr. (son b. 1909) 46

Roosevelt, Franklin, Jr. (son b. 1914) 48, 49, 53, 78, 92

Roosevelt, Franklin Delano (husband)

health 47, 48, 50, 53–57, 59–60, 64, 93

life 34–43, 95–97

play about 110

political career 46–53, 64, 66–79, 94–95

Roosevelt, Hall (brother) 15, 17, 18, 22–24, 32, 88

Roosevelt, James (son) 45, 48, 53, 76, 78, 92, 94

Roosevelt, John (son) 48, 49, 53, 63, 78, 92

Roosevelt, Sara Delano (mother-in-law) 36–40, 43, 44, 53, 82, 87–88

Roosevelt, Theodore "Teddy" (uncle) 9, 15, 22, 24–25, 32, 35, 41

Souvestre, Marie 26–28, 29–30, 31, 33, 41

Soviet Union 94, 95, 99, 106–107

tenements 8, 21, 35, 40, 62, 77, 79, 83

Thompson, Malvina "Tommy" 71, 72, 91, 92, 111–112

Truman, Pres. Harry 96–97, 98, 119, 120

unemployment 64, 65, 70, 73, 75, 77

United Nations

Amer. Assoc. for the U. N. 108, 113, 116

Eleanor as delegate 98, 102, 105, 119, 121

founding 95

Human Rights Commission 99–101, 102, 121

women's issues 36–37, 53, 57–58, 70–71, 82, 105, 117

women's rights 47, 53, 61

worker's rights 36–37, 57–58

World War II 84, 85–95, 97–98, 105

Organizations of Interest

Visit the Eleanor Roosevelt National Historic Site at Val-Kill in Hyde Park, New York. It remains much the way Eleanor left it in 1962. (www.nps.gov/elro/)

Across the road in Hyde Park, you will find the Home of Franklin D. Roosevelt National Historic Site (www.nps.gov/hofr/). Visit the house Sara shared with Franklin and Eleanor, the beautiful grounds, and the FDR Library and Museum (www.fdrlibrary.marist.edu).

In Washington, D. C., the Franklin Delano Roosevelt Memorial, with its dramatic statuary and inscriptions, is a testament to the contributions made by both Franklin and Eleanor. (www.nps.gov/fdrm)

The "First Ladies: Political Role and Public Image" exhibit at the Smithsonian National Museum of American History, also in Washington, provides a fascinating look at Eleanor and other first ladies. (http://americanhistory.si.edu)

You will find valuable information about Eleanor's human rights work on the Web site titled "The Eleanor Roosevelt Papers: The Human Rights Years, 1945-1962," at www.gwu.edu/~erpapers/.

Acknowledgments

Many thanks to all who made this book possible: to the staff at the FDR Library, including Bob Clark, Virginia Lewick, Mark Renovitch, and Alycia Vivona; to Diane Lobb-Boyce at the Eleanor Roosevelt National Historic Site at Val-Kill; to Mary Bain, who worked for the National Youth Administration in Chicago and became a friend to Eleanor Roosevelt; to Wayne Kempton, archivist at the Cathedral of St. John the Divine; to Miriam Cohen, Professor of History, Vassar College, for her careful reading and excellent suggestions; to my thoughtful and perceptive editor Stephanie Smith; to Kate, Eve, Ida, Brian, and Dan for all their help; to my husband Jon for his insight and encouragement; and to Lucille and Carl Harris who, a long time ago, gave a copy of *Eleanor Roosevelt: Her Day* to our three daughters.

Picture Credits

The photographs in this book are used with permission and through the courtesy of: (t=top; b=bottom; l=left; r=right; c=center; a=above) Corbis: pp.1-2 title page, 25,34,35,36,49,52,54,62, 64,66-67,68,74,82,83,84,90-91,97b,106,110,120 Bettman; p.8 Jose F. Poblete; p.23t Lake County Museum; p.27,80,86-87 Hulton Deutsch Collection; p.30 Fine Art Photographic Library; p.47,90t Corbis; p.81 Royalty Free;p.104 Kamal Kishore/Reuters; White House Historical Society:pp.3,123br; UN/DPI:pp.5,101,123tr; Franklin D. Roosevelt Library:pp.7,9,10,11,12-13,15,16,18-19,20, 22-23,24,26,28,29,31,32,33,37,38,39,40,41,42,44,45,46,48,51,53,56,58t,60,61,63,67t,69,70,71,72, 73,76,77,88,89,92,93t,93b,94,96-97,98-99,102-103,105,107,108,111,114,115,117,122(all),123 bl; AP/Wide World Photos:pp.58-59,121; National Archives:p.65,123tl; West Virginia and Regional History Collection/West Virginia University Libraries:p.75; Library of Congress:pp.78-79,113; Dr. A. David Gurewitsch:pp.112,118; Getty Images:p.116 Edward Hausner/New York Times Co.; BORDER PHOTOS from left to right: Corbis; Corbis/Bettman; Corbis/Bettman; Corbis/Bettman; Denver Public Library; Franklin D. Roosevelt Library; Corbis/David J.& Janice L. Frent Library; Corbis/ Bettman; Franklin D. Roosevelt Library; Franklin D. Roosevelt Library; Corbis Sygma/Ellis Richard; Library of Congress; Corbis/Bettman

Author's Note

In the course of my research, I visited several places where Eleanor Roosevelt had lived and worked, as well as the FDR Library in Hyde Park. I also found several human rights organizations that work to achieve the goals to which Eleanor Roosevelt aspired:

Amnesty International promotes research and action to prevent and end abuses to human rights. (www.amnesty.org)
Human Rights Watch works to prevent discrimination, stop human rights abuses in war, and bring offenders to justice. (www.hrw.org)
United Nations Children's Fund (UNICEF) works to improve the education, health, nutrition, and protection of children. (www.unicef.org)

DK Biography: *Albert Einstein*
by Frieda Wishinsky
ISBN 0-7566-1247-0 paperback
ISBN 0-7566-1248-9 hardcover

DK Biography: *Anne Frank*
by Kem Knapp Sawyer
ISBN 0-7566-0341-2 paperback
ISBN 0-7566-0490-7 hardcover

DK Biography: *Helen Keller*
by Leslie Garrett
ISBN 0-7566-0339-0 paperback
ISBN 0-7566-0488-5 hardcover

DK Biography: *John F. Kennedy*
by Howard S. Kaplan
ISBN 0-7566-0340-4 paperback
ISBN 0-7566-0489-3 hardcover

DK Biography: *Martin Luther King, Jr.*
by Amy Pastan
ISBN 0-7566-0342-0 paperback
ISBN 0-7566-0491-5 hardcover

DK Biography: *Abraham Lincoln*
by Tanya Lee Stone
ISBN 0-7566-0341-2 paperback
ISBN 0-7566-0490-7 hardcover

DK Biography: *George Washington*
by Lenny Hort
ISBN 0-7566-0835-X paperback
ISBN 0-7566-0832-5 hardcover

DK Biography: *Princess Diana*
by Joanne Mattern
ISBN 0-7566-1614-X paperback
ISBN 0-7566-1613-1 hardcover

Look what the critics are saying about DK Biography!

"…highly readable, worthwhile overviews for young people…"—*Booklist*

"This new series from the inimitable DK Publishing brings together the usual brilliant photography with a historian's approach to biography subjects."
—*Ingram Library Services*